SOCIOLOGY

An Outline for the Intending Student

CONTRIBUTORS

G. Duncan Mitchell

Margaret Hewitt

Anne Crichton

James Littlejohn

David M. Barkla

Howard Jones

Albert B. Cherns

SOCIOLOGY

An Outline for the Intending Student

Edited by

Professor G. Duncan Mitchell

Head of the Department of Sociology
University of Exeter

LONDON

ROUTLEDGE & KEGAN PAUL

First published 1970
by Routledge & Kegan Paul Ltd
Broadway House, 68-74 Carter Lane
London, E.C.4
Printed in Great Britain
by Willmer Brothers Limited
Birkenhead, Cheshire
ISBN 0 7100 6842 5 (C)
ISBN 0 7100 6843 3 (P)

CONTENTS

ACKNOWLEDGMENTS

The Editor wishes to thank the following publishers for permission to quote from the works listed below:

George Allen and Unwin for *Sociology: a Guide to Problems and Literature* by T. B. Bottomore and *The Elementary Forms of Religious Life* by Durkheim, tr. by J. W. Swain; Harvard University Press for *Beyond Nationalization* by G. B. Baldwin; Longmans Green for *English Social History* by G. M. Trevelyan; the Macmillan Company, New York for *Human Society* by Kingsley Davis and *Social Structure* by G. P. Murdock; Oxford University Press for *The Professions* by Sir Alexander Carr-Saunders and P. A. Wilson; Prentice-Hall International for *The World of Work* by R. Dubin and *Professionalization* by H. L. Vollmer and D. M. Mills; Tavistock Publications Ltd. for the Tavistock Institute of Human Relations for *Family and Social Network* by Elizabeth Bott and *Social Research and a National Policy for Science* (Tavistock Publication No. 7).

I

Introduction

G. Duncan Mitchell

It is sometimes said that Sociology is a new, or young, subject and there is some truth in this. Certainly, as far as its place in universities is concerned it is fairly new. Few chairs of sociology were in existence in European universities before the Second World War. The earliest in Britain was established in London University in 1907. In the U.S.A., however, there were departments in some universities and colleges before the First World War, but the great expansion came in the inter-war period and immediately afterwards. However, if we look outside academic institutions and examine the writers of the nineteenth century we may discover quite a large number of prominent scholars who have contributed to the subject, among whom we may mention Auguste Comte and Herbert Spencer. We can go further back into history and argue that the subject has grown into a recognizable branch of learning, slowly perhaps, but clearly definable although not under its present name, since Charles Secondat, Baron de la Brède et de Montesquieu wrote his famous book *De l'esprit des lois* in 1748. The term *sociology* came much later and was coined by Auguste Comte in the 1830s to describe the new science of society. One reason why sociology appears to be new is because it has only been in the past ten to fifteen years that large numbers of young people have wanted to study it at university for a first degree, or as part of one. It is for such aspirants to places in universities that this book has been written; its purpose is to inform the

1

intending student so that he or she may know more of what the subject is about.

In this Introduction we shall first of all say a little more about the newness of the subject because it is important to know why it came into existence when it did. We shall indicate the relationship of sociology to other cognate disciplines, and then say something general about the various parts and aspects of the subject by way of introducing the accounts given in subsequent chapters. These chapters aim to give a brief survey of branches of the subject and to indicate trends in thought, together with some of the principal findings of the researches that have been undertaken.

Firstly, let us consider the origins of the subject. Why did it come into existence when it did and why has it been only in recent decades that it has flourished in universities? To answer these questions is not easy but the argument offered here will both attempt to do so and also help to place sociology in the scheme of modern studies.

Sociology, like some other social studies such as economics, psychology and history, was forged in the crucible of that late eighteenth-century period in European history we call the *Enlightenment*. In part, this historical phenomenon was a result of the development and application of the ideas of the early scientists in the seventeenth century whose belief that the physical world could be explained in terms of a number of laws excited men to speculation. For the next two hundred years these ideas enthralled many thinkers in France, and what we now call Germany, as they had caught the imagination of that group of Englishmen who founded the Royal Society of London in 1662. In part, and not altogether unconnected with this, we may discern another factor. This was a fundamental change in attitude amongst educated people, especially in France, toward social institutions. Traditionally it had been held that some, if not all, of the institutions of society were of divine origin or were divinely ordained. Certainly the Church came into this category and also the Monarchy, with the implication that it was impious to question them, even when they manifestly were failing to meet specific social needs or proved, in some respect, to be inefficient. It was Montesquieu who led the way to a fresh view, for in a book he wrote in 1734 about the ancient world, entitled *Considérations sur les Causes de la Grandeur des Romaines et de leur Décadence,* he applied for the first time the modern scientific method, as it was then understood, to historical data. Indeed, he analysed the institutions of ancient Rome in a novel way, showing how the rise and fall of empires is attributable to general causes of a moral or a physical nature, but not either to blind chance or to divine intervention. In his subsequent and better known work which we referred to earlier, *De l'esprit des lois,* he investigated more specifically the nature of the laws governing human social events and human behaviour with particular respect to social institutions, as well as providing a discussion of the nature of laws of the kind that are the concern of the courts. Now we should make it clear that this was not the beginning of historical studies, but it was the beginning of a fresh outlook on history, one which may perhaps be seen among some of the ancient Greek historians, but which had not been noticeable for many centuries and which was, in the context of the ideas and beliefs of the time, quite a novelty.

The example Montesquieu set influenced many other thinkers, especially in France, and thus social institutions came to be both analysed and criticized, among them political and educational institutions, and this development had far-reaching results. It may be seen in the works of Voltaire, Diderot, D'Alembert, Condorcet and St Simon as well as many others, including that redoubtable lady, Madame de Staël; it was a ferment of ideas and political events which, spread over a period of fifty years, came to be known as the French Revolution, that signal occasion when a nation endeavoured to abolish its old order to recreate in new forms its principal social institutions: political, religious, legal, familial and educational.

It is no exaggeration to say that the Revolutionary movement in France inspired the development of sociology, not because it was revolutionary in the sense of wishing to overturn the existing order, but because it represented an outlook

3

on the part of men which legitimated the open and frank examination of society, an outlook which entertained criticisms of the various parts and their working and which allowed for the proposal of new forms by way of reconstruction. If the Comte Henri de St Simon was a socialist, Auguste Comte was not; but both, despite their differences, made assumptions which would not have been possible before Montesquieu. We have emphasized the influence of developments in France on the beginnings of sociology but it was not purely a French product. Comte had a strong influence on John Stuart Mill, with whom he was in correspondence, and Mill's ideas have been powerful in Britain, and he also influenced Herbert Spencer. However, even before Comte there were stirrings of a sociological nature in Scotland, as may be seen in the writings of John Millar and Adam Ferguson, and in Germany there were the writings of Gottfried von Herder, different again but contributing to this type of thought. To discuss all these writers would mean embarking on another book. Let it suffice to say that the study of social institutions, either in order to discern their lawful order and change or with a view to effecting changes, is a relatively novel aspect of modern western culture, and that this has largely been the source of the organized body of knowledge we now call sociology.

To answer the question why the subject has flourished so greatly in academic courses of study in recent years is less easy, but we may note the attempt, since the Second World War, to re-examine our social institutions afresh, to see to what extent changes are desirable in the light of modern technological advances, and to review the changing needs of a country which is no longer the centre of a great empire but is in competition with many other highly industrialized nations. The demands for skills and for awakened and trained ability and intelligence, the necessity to utilize more fully the human resources of our society, and the desire for greater egalitarianism in our system of education seem to be among the causal factors which have led governments to seek sociological assistance in formulating policies for educational reform, for improving relationships between management and labour, for discerning the organizational factors that lead to industrial disputes, and for producing ideas relevant to the planning of new towns and the redevelopment of old ones so that benefits accrue to the inhabitants and therefore unrest, crime and delinquency are reduced. In short, sociology is seen to be useful, or at least potentially useful.

In addition to being useful, sociology is perceived to be a necessary adjunct to other studies. More and more, sociology is recognized as offering a vantage-point to the historian, who may with this advantage examine the course of events with a keener eye for social, rather than military, diplomatic or political factors. Again, it is clear that the economist's assumptions about 'economic man' do not hold entirely and that some of the aspects of human behaviour which the sociologist selects for study are relevant to an understanding of consumption patterns and the operation of the market. Or again, the psychologist may well be able to shed light on the behaviour of the individual, but the individual cannot, without great error, be regarded in isolation from his social environment, and so the psychologist's work is complemented by that of the social psychologist, who is usually more of a sociologist than a psychologist in training and outlook.

We should not be obsessed by academic boundaries and some universities have tried to minimize them to the point of risking the introduction of confusion in an endeavour to avoid the dangers inherent in drawing dividing lines, but there are some distinctions which it is important to make. Thus we should point out that sociology is neither an aspect of history, nor of economics, nor of psychology, although there are close relationships between sociology and these disciplines. It is a way of looking at human behaviour, as they are also; but it has its own particular approach, its own language and, above all, it asks its own distinctive questions. But it is a branch of knowledge clearly related to these disciplines and no-one can be a successful sociologist who does not know some history, economics and psychology. Briefly, let us now consider the kinds of questions the sociologist asks, noting the ways in which they differ from those asked by a person studying another social science.

Historians, of course, differ among themselves a great deal in their interests. Some write a narrative kind of history, relating a series of events; they may do so with an interest in military and diplomatic facts, or have political or economic or social interests in their subject. Others write biographical history focusing the attention of the reader on a particular figure like Elizabeth I, Oliver Cromwell or Napoleon Bonaparte, and in doing so they bring out in discussion the personal influence of the character they have chosen as it bore on policy-making. Some historians have looked at an entire civilization or a lengthy period of European history in order to discern major trends, to analyse the causes of the rise and fall of empires or important institutions. Since Montesquieu there have been many famous writers: Gibbon, Niebuhr and Mommsen on the Roman Empire, Delisle Burns on early Europe, Voltaire on the age of Louis XIV, de Tocqueville on *L'Ancien Régime et la Revolution* and, in addition, since Hegel's early attempt at writing world history, the works of Oswald Spengler and A. J. Toynbee. These last two are not always viewed with much favour by professional historians for they distrust generalization and their positivist philosophy discourages them from making the attempt. But Toynbee, especially, may be said to come nearer than most of them (although de Tocqueville is another but rather different case too) to the sociological approach, for he examines social structures and institutions, and above all he treats his material comparatively.

Economists too vary greatly in their interests. Some are theorists, putting forward general statements about the way the economy works. They make certain kinds of assumptions about human nature and try to build up, by stages of increasing complexity, a picture of economic relationships. In this manner they show how demand and supply are related and how prices are determined. They examine the monetary system to show the nature of the relationship between the parts; rate of interest, quantity of money in circulation, level of employment and so forth. There is a similarity here with the work of some sociologists who are interested in abstract theoretical formulations, and who try to put forward models of social relations of increasing complexity from simple beginnings in the hope that in this way they will more clearly understand the inter-relationships of that coherence we call society.

The psychologist studies human behaviour. Often he believes that by experiments with animals he can determine laws of behaviour and that this will enable him to infer something about human behaviour. Doubtless, on the level of simple stimulus-response behaviour he may do so, but of course he has to face the scepticism of those who argue that human beings do reflect, display imagination and exercise their wills in ways that are not usual among the lower forms of animal life. And there are others who are less inclined to value experimental methods in this field, believing that clinical observations are more valuable, and who try to develop arguments about the nature and genesis of personality, describing the structure of personality, its various parts and their inter-relationships. Such has been the work of Sigmund Freud and the many other people who have been inspired by his work and written in the tradition of psychoanalysis and its variant forms.

However, the sociologist is neither an historian, an economist nor a psychologist. He is interested in the data of history but emphasizes structures of relationships rather than narratives of events; he examines economies, but not to determine economic principles so much as to see the links between say, a type of economy and a type of family and kinship system; he looks at human behaviour to see a relationship between a method of education and the resultant personality type, or between the nature of group membership and the development of attitudes. Essentially, the sociologist asks a question about the social structure, and the norms and values which govern the behaviour of people, for we should realize that people choose to behave in ways which are for the most part prescribed; we fulfil our own, and other people's, expectations and we do so many, many more times than not—we are all conformists. Even those who fail to conform in important respects, like criminals whom we put in prison or the insane whom we incarcerate in asylums, usually conform rather than otherwise, although the areas of life in which conformity obtains are apparently so commonplace as to blind us to the fact. We eat, work and sleep in regular patterns, we obey numerous rules as we cross roads, buy goods in shops, use the telephone, borrow books from the library, and greet our neighbours. It is this structure of social life, its norms, the relationships we enter into, the behaviour we manifest collectively that is the subject matter of the sociologist. Clearly, some of the behaviour is economic in character or has implications for the economist; it is the behaviour of humans and therefore the raw material of the historian and the psychologist, but it is behaviour looked at in a certain way; in short, the kind of abstraction employed differs from that of the economist and the psychologist, although both, like the sociologist, are concerned with human behaviour.

Let us now proceed to examine more closely the nature of the abstractions the sociologist employs and his reasons for doing so. Only in this way will we really come to grips with the subject and understand what the sociologist is doing and why. Probably the most important intellectual tool in the sociologist's kit is the idea of society as a *system*. Many departments of knowledge make use of this idea. Thus the crystallographer studies a crystal as a system of molecules, and a physiologist regards an organism as a system of cells. Of course, the unit members of the system may vary in their characteristics. A mechanical system, like a bicycle, consists of various and different mechanical parts, and the monetary system, as we mentioned earlier, has different ingredients. But the point of utilizing the idea of a system is to point to the inter-relationships between the parts which make up the whole. A society may therefore be regarded as a system of *social institutions,* e.g. economy, kinship, law and custom, government, education, religion and so forth, and the sociologist endeavours to trace the relationships between these various parts. In so far as it is useful to employ this idea it follows that changes in a part of a system will have repercussions on other parts. To be sure, if we alter the nature of our economy we shall have to adjust our educational policies; today some people are saying a lot about this and arguing that the technological changes in the British economy require a greater emphasis on technological instruction with consequently greater emphasis on science in schools. Others are inclined to argue that what we need today are better managers and executives, skilled in handling people as well as in planning for the future, and that the social sciences, sociology especially, deserve to be given greater resources to meet the needs of an advanced industrial society. In the study of developing countries the relationship between economy and kinship is of great importance, especially where man's livelihood depends in large measure on a peasant economy which utilizes family labour and where credit is obtained from kinsfolk.

The idea of a system applied to social phenomena may be employed on a different level from the one we have mentioned. In most cases of sociological research something less than a total society is taken for the field of study or even something less ambitious than a social institution. It may be that the sociologist is interested to examine not the institution of education as a whole, but a school, not the economy in relation to kinship, but a firm, and in these cases he is examining a *social organization*. But he may nevertheless regard his organization as a social system—in this case a social system of persons occupying *positions* in the organization, such positions being defined in terms of rights and duties, expectations and obligations, or in short by *norms*, in terms of which those persons who occupy such positions act in certain ways, or as we say they play *roles*. Here again the sociologist is keen to discern the relationships between the parts which make up the whole. Sometimes the sociologist looks at an even smaller social phenomenon, a small group; it may be a group of workers at a bench in a workshop, or a class of school children, or an army platoon. Here the idea of a social system is still useful, but of course the sociologist has repeatedly to ask himself if he is not placing too much

9

weight on this idea. Is a social organization or a group as integrated as the idea of it being a system suggests?

The plan of this book, whose purpose is to inform the intending student of the subject, follows this general kind of discussion. Thus we have a chapter on social institutions, one on social organizations and another on social groups. In this manner we indicate the kinds of topics sociologists are interested in and in so doing we show how his interest may dwell on macro-sociological topics or on micro-sociological ones, i.e. on large-scale or small-scale social systems.

The foregoing discussion illustrates one further aspect of sociology, for whilst one may examine a particular social institution, organization or group, and by analysing and describing it discover its nature, it is also possible to make comparisons. Thus the sociologist may wish to compare kinship systems, as did the late A. R. Radcliffe-Brown, and discern some principles governing their formation and structure. He may wish to compare different systems of child-rearing, not only to discover how personality may be variously conditioned, but in order to examine the ways in which a method of child-rearing is articulated with the educational system. In this connection, for example, it would be instructive to compare the French and American systems of child-rearing and relate them to the educational institutions of those two countries; much may be learned about the differing emphases in values in each case. Comparison is of the very essence of sociological enquiry, and there are many reasons for this. In the first place it is desirable to perceive one's own culture or society in perspective; that is to say, to view it with some detachment, to avoid partisan views and to achieve some measure of objectivity. The sociologist who studies only his own society, or aspects of it, with no reference to other societies is failing to reap the main advantage the subject offers him. Moreover, he will soon fail to appreciate the more subtle aspects of his own society's beliefs and values; he will suffer the fate of being parochial and narrow. However, there is another reason which we must stress: in order that sociology may develop, it must transcend pure description, however necessary this is in the first instance, and proceed to analysis and comparison, for unless there is comparison there can be no generalization, no principles governing social structures will be discerned, the lawful order of human existence, the whole point of sociological thought will be missed. It is not easy to carry out comparative studies, to compare only what is comparable, to discern the similarities among the differences, to bring order into seeming chaos without forcing the categories or falsifying the evidence; all this is the task, and a difficult task, of the sociologist who wishes to advance his subject nor merely by adding to it, but by developing it.

Fundamentally, we may say that the sociologist is making a study of the structure of society, or some particular aspect of it, at a moment in time, tracing the inter-relationships and seeking to understand the sociological principles underlying the social order. But sometimes the sociologist is concerned to look at the way a social structure changes over a period of time. He wants to know if the structure is of such a kind that there are inherent factors predisposing it to change, indeed, possibly determining changes along predictable lines. Here we have a view that has been inspired by (*inter alia*) Karl Marx, who described the essential features of capitalism in such a way as to show, to his own and his adherents' satisfaction anyway, that it contained within itself the seeds of its own dissolution. Today we are rather more interested perhaps to trace the course of industrialization, comparing the processes in various countries, to see the principles governing its development. Order and change are both fundamental focal points for the sociologist, but they are not antithetical approaches, for one can hardly study order without reference to change, and vice versa.

It is sometimes thought that sociologists turn their attention to the disorderly features of their society, to crime, alchoholism, drug addiction, divorce and so forth; and, to be sure, some do specialize in this way. To this end we have included a chapter on *social deviance* by Professor Howard Jones, himself a distinguished criminologist. But it should not be supposed that this is the prime function of sociology. There are more people studying the normal forms of be-

11

haviour than the abnormal ones. This is entirely reasonable, for the sociologist is not, as such, a social worker, a reformer or engaged in political and administrative matters. The sociologist is a student of human behaviour in its collective and structural aspects. He has to be detached and observant rather than engaged or committed to policies or political activity, although this is not precluded. Even if he sees sociology as being useful and capable of application to the end of improving the society he belongs to, he realizes that it is first necessary to consider carefully the kind of society he is interested to improve. He has to be mainly devoted to understanding the way it works, to discerning the nature of the values and norms which govern people's behaviour and to account for them taking the forms they do. Thus, primarily, the sociologist is the student of everyday behaviour; that which is standard and constant. It is only when the basis has been laid for an understanding of society as it exists that he may proceed to examine the aberrant features of human behaviour and seek understanding of deviance with some hope of success. Having said this we should perhaps add that university Departments of Sociology do tend to vary a little in their emphases; some are more interested in the 'problems' of society than others, some emphasize the importance of empirical studies, often small in scale, as a means of building up a body of useful knowledge about our society; other departments tend to be more contemplative and value the philosophical and historical aspects of the subject. The intending student will want to know something of the major interests of the staff of a university department, but he should realize that despite these differences there is a very great deal that sociologists have in common, and that what they have in common is an interest in building up a body of coherent knowledge about the structural aspects of human behaviour as they may be observed.

Most university courses for honours students permit some specialization. Some students, for example, are interested in urban sociological studies, other in industrial relations, some wish to know about criminology and deviance, others about a specific institution like religion or kinship. Indeed, there has developed a tendency for specific institutions to be the subjects for courses and a number of branches of the subject have grown up, each having an extensive literature. This is particularly the case with the sociology of education, political sociology and the sociology of marriage and the family, but sociology of religion and urban and rural sociology also feature prominently in university courses and these are discussed in the chapter by Dr Margaret Hewitt, herself a scholar who specializes in the sociology of the family and of religion. Two other identifiable aspects of the subject are represented in this book. One is concerned with studies of small communities and the other with the study of small groups; these essays into the sphere of micro-sociology deserve some comment.

The study of the small community is essentially something which has been developed by social anthropologists, that is to say those sociologists who mainly study simple societies, often in the past pre-literate societies, but today more often developing societies such as those in Africa. Ethnographic studies are essentially descriptive and often descriptive of a social whole. Thus social anthropologists have made studies of the culture and social structure of an entire tribal people such as the Basuto or the Kipsigis of Africa or the inhabitants of the Pacific island of Tikopia. Some sociologists who have taken an interest in African peoples have examined the life of such people in an urban setting, but in each case they have been investigating the structure of community.

In modern industrial societies sociologists, often inspired by these studies by social anthropologists, have turned their attention to rural communities on the periphery of Britain's industrial areas and the communities found in small mining or manufacturing towns, sometimes even those embedded in large metropolitan areas. An example of the last kind is the work of M. Young and P. Willmott and other members of the Institute of Community Studies in London, but the tradition is older than this, for in the 1930s similar work was being done by the sociologists of the University of Chicago under the inspiration of Robert Park, and sociologists all over the world have felt the need to make studies of local communities, and usually, in the process, to reflect on just what is meant by the term *community*. One of the origins of this tradition lies in Germany in the work of Ferdinand Tönnies in Kiel fifty years ago and it is still being continued in that country today by Rene König and others. In Britain it has especially flourished since the Second World War in the study of residential neighbourhoods and thus it is part of urban sociology. On this subject Dr James Littlejohn, himself both social anthropologist and sociologist, has written a chapter in this book.

The study of small groups grew out of social psychology and is chiefly an American product. It was a development which lent itself to some experimental work, an unusual feature of sociology, and it may be said to have enjoyed some theoretical success. Clearly, it links up with some studies of small communities, and it has had considerable applications, as Mr David M. Barkla shows in his chapter on this subject.

Applied sociology having been mentioned, it remains to say that this book contains a chapter on the subject. It is dangerous to claim too much for sociology, as some have done, and sociology has suffered from the disappointments of those who, usually ignorant of it, nevertheless have hoped for too much from it. But there are some realms in which sociological knowledge can be useful. Merely to offer explanations of human behaviour is sometimes sufficient to make policy-makers pause to consider again the probable consequences of their actions. Administrators never have sufficient information and policies are frequently devised on assumptions that have not been tested and, to be fair, often cannot be tested without inordinate expense of time and money. But sociologists may well reduce the degree of uncertainty and risk attendant on policy-making if they are encouraged to do so. Professor A. B. Cherns, who has had considerable and extensive experience in the administration of government finance for social research, has contributed a special chapter which indicates the present scope and limits of the applicability of sociology.

Little has been said so far about training in research techniques. The professional sociologist, however, is a person

14

possessing certain skills. Firstly, there are intellectual skills which enable him to formulate a problem, to make the necessary distinctions and establish categories of thought permitting the adequate analysis and discussion of the problem and which allow him to plan a course of investigation or enquiry designed to shed light on the problem. Secondly, and as part of this, many research projects require of him that he should have the skill or technical expertise to enable him to cast the problem selected in a form permitting the application of tests. His hypotheses should be operationally defined so that empirical tests may be applied, and this very often entails the employment of quantifiable techniques. In this connection much sociological research today requires the knowledge of how to plan a social survey and how to assess the results of the survey in terms of statistical methods. It sometimes happens that the knowledge that this is an important part of an honours course in sociology puts a candidate off, but it should be remembered that the degree of mathematical training required is not very great. A candidate with an Ordinary Level pass in the G.C.E. examination in mathematics should be capable of successfully achieving the necessary level of understanding of the elementary statistical methodology that most sociology courses require. It is not necessary for a sociologist to have a very detailed and intensive knowledge of statistics, but it is a part of his equipment that he should be reasonably numerate as well as literate. There are, of course, other ingredients in sociological methods courses besides a knowledge of elementary statistical methods and among them are the planning of questionnaires and the formulation of questions, interviewing techniques, coding results and the use of data-processing machinery.

The intending student of sociology should want to know how he can use his degree in the subject. Of course, he may be so interested and sufficiently competent in pursuing the study of the subject that he aims to take up a career of research and teaching in it, and to be sure, there are a number of openings in universities, technical colleges and colleges of further education. Teacher training colleges also look for socio-

logists, but it is highly desirable that in addition to a qualification in the subject a candidate for a post in this kind of
institution should have had a training as a teacher and some
experience in a school as such. There are, however, a number
of other careers for which a degree in sociology is useful.
Firstly we should mention social administration and social
work. Here we refer mainly to local government and to the
child care, probation, medical social work, mental health and
welfare services in particular, but also include the housing
departments. A degree is a useful background but it is recommended that a candidate for a post in social work should
take a special professional course afterwards. Some generic
courses offered by a number of universities are designed to
the end of taking selected social science graduates and putting them through a tailor-made course to give them the
professional skills and experience required. Another type of
local government position which sociology graduates can
compete for is found in planning departments, for whilst
these posts have traditionally tended to go to geography
graduates and to those qualified in surveying or with a
degree in engineering or architecture, there is an increasing
willingness on the part of the more advanced and larger
planning departments to include a sociologist or two. Indeed, there are a few town-planning courses in universities
which take sociologists and give them the extra qualification
and this is highly desirable.

By and large, of course, graduates in sociology go on to do
a variety of things, many of them unclassifiable. The fact is
that a degree in sociology, like an arts degree, has little direct
relevance to occupations other than those of teaching or
researching in the subject. Perhaps it has a little greater
background relevance in a few cases, e.g. market research
and administration. But of course it is a degree which indicates to the future employer that the candidate is of an
enquiring mind; interested in the social world around him;
knowledgeable about some aspects of it; possibly skilled in
some quantitative techniques, or at least not afraid to look at
a table of statistics and find it conveys information; a
person with a trained mind capable of wending his or her

way through the common prejudices that all too often pass for common sense, to bring some precision of thought into a matter concerning human relationships; someone who has been trained to view social situations with a measure of detachment without losing human sympathy. In short, the qualities that are essential for the administrator are likely to be brought out in an honours course in sociology and such an academic background may well commend itself to a prospective employer; it will do so especially if the candidate can talk sensibly and with insight about the nature of administrative decision-making and the problem of putting over a policy change to those whose lives are likely to be affected by it. (See Appendix II.)

However, when we have said all this it must be added that some young people will want to study sociology because they are curious about man and his society, about the human condition and the social world that has produced it and which is man's inheritance and his challenge, and these people should study the subject because they find it an end in itself, self-justifying and an intellectually desirable way in which the human spirit may be manifested.

SUGGESTED READING

MITCHELL, G. Duncan, *A Hundred Years of Sociology* (Duckworth, 1968, Pb. 1970).

INKELES, Alex, *What is Sociology?* (New York: Prentice-Hall, 1964).

A work of reference containing both definitions and explanations of sociological concepts is *A Dictionary of Sociology*, edited by G. Duncan Mitchell, 1968, Routledge & Kegan Paul.

Other introductory texts published in paperback editions are:

GOLDTHORPE, J. E., *An Introduction to Sociology* (C.U.P., 1968).

BOTTOMORE, T. B., *Sociology, a Guide to Problems and Literature* (Allen & Unwin, 1962).

MITCHELL, G. Duncan, *Sociology: the Study of Social Systems* (University Tutorial Press, 1966, Revised Edition 1970).

COTGROVE, S., *The Science of Society: an Introduction to Sociology* (Allen & Unwin, 1967).

2

Social Institutions

Margaret Hewitt

What is a social institution? Here, as so frequently in sociology, we are confronted with a number of definitions and
usages. Not all of them are immediately intelligible even to
those reasonably acquainted with the jargon of academic
sociologists. W. G. Sumner, for example, asserts that:

> an institution consists of a concept (idea, notion, doctrine,
> interest) and a structure.... The structure is a framework,
> or apparatus, or perhaps only a number of functionaries.
> ... [It] holds the concept and furnishes instrumentalities
> for bringing it into the world of facts and action....[1]

Nor, it must be admitted, do sociologists always use the term
consistently in the light of their own definition—as Sumner's
own work well illustrates. The need for a clarification of the
concept of social institution is indeed discussed in some
detail by H. E. Smith in *Sociology and Social Research,*
1964. Nevertheless, on one thing most sociologists are basically agreed : social institutions are socially approved patterns
of social relationships. Morris Ginsberg in *Sociology,* 1934,
writes that social institutions are recognized and established
usages governing the relations between individuals and
groups and R. M. MacIver and C. H. Page, in *Society,*
1949, define them as 'established forms or conditions of
procedure characteristic of group activity'. It is important to
recognize in such a definition of social institution that the
corollary of social approval is social disapproval and social
sanctions against individuals who deviate from the recog-

nized behaviour pattern. Social institutions are thus not merely an expression of what *is* done in a particular situation in a particular society; they also operate to determine what *ought* to be done. They are therefore part of the normative order of a society and as such are a means of social control.

There are, of course, other types of norm which operate as social controls and it is important to distinguish between these and the particular norms in which we are interested, social institutions. There are so many distinctions here that cut across one another that systematic classification is difficult. One way is to differentiate norms on the basis of the kind of sanctions applied. Some rules are supported merely by wild disapproval of the violator, while others are supported by physical force. This distinction is correlated to some extent with the degree of importance attached to the rule in society and with the manner by which the rule comes into being (whether by deliberate legislation or by unconscious growth). Finally, there is a slight correlation between these criteria and the degree of spontaneity with which the rule is followed as well as the rapidity with which the rule changes. These correlations, however, are very rough. What sociologists have done is simply to group norms into several broad classes, admitting that the various criteria of distinction overlap considerably and that the classification is therefore crude. In this way they usually distinguish what are called folkways, mores and law.

Most of the patterns appplied in everyday behaviour consist of folkways. These are relatively durable, standardized practices regarded as obligatory in the proper situation, but not absolutely obligatory, enforced by informal social controls (gossip, ridicule, ostracism) rather than by formal complaint or coercion, and originating in an unplanned and obscure manner rather than by deliberate inauguration :

The number of meals we eat a day, the kinds of food chosen, the use of tables and chairs rather than squatting on rugs on the floor—all these are folkways. It is through the folkways that the business of living is made possible for human beings, and their unreflecting character makes

19

for efficiency and frees our minds for the more problematical events of life. Many folkways are repeated so often in the daily routine of individuals and groups that they become habits—habits of thought as well as action—and they come to form 'the unstated premises in our mental life'.[2]

They thus provide a high degree of predictability both of our own and of others' behaviour, so that we feel some security and order in life. It is this feeling of security which our own folkways provide which makes foreign travel so exciting for some—and so daunting for the less intrepid. 'Strange' food, 'strange' habits are the small-change of highly-coloured accounts of the past summer's travels abroad. Differences of language—itself, as Kingsley Davis points out, 'a system of verbal folkways'—surprise and discomfort those who hope to make themselves understood thousands of miles from the cliffs of Dover by the simple expedient of speaking English increasingly loudly to the uncomprehending 'native'. Yet English, like other languages, is in essence an arbitrary selection of sounds and combinations of sounds which have been selected by a particular society and made to apply to particular objects and ideas so that its members may communicate with one another by means of sound. That other societies have chosen other sets of sounds to communicate the same idea, though inconvenient for those unfamiliar with these languages, is neither a reflection on their intelligence nor on their integrity. Indeed, unwillingness to acquaint oneself with the language of one's hosts is frequently interpreted by them as a deliberate discourtesy.

To violate some of the folkways of one's own or some other society is usually possible—one can drink coffee at 'tea-time' —but it is impossible to violate all of them, for then the individual would find himself virtually excluded from social contact. Survival would then be extremely difficult, not merely from an external or physical point of view, but also from an internal or mental point of view. For the individual in question, the very reasons for nonconformity in one particular situation are apt to be the folkways in most other situations in which he finds himself, as the bizarre attire of certain groups of young, or would-be young people, of our own day well illustrates.

The sanctions of the folkways are themselves folkways, and are by definition comparatively mild, consisting generally in informal retaliations such as direct or indirect expressions of adverse opinions. It follows from this that to be effective, the individual against whom the sanctions are directed must himself be a member of the group within which the violated folkway operates. The icy stares of the regular congregation are unlikely to suppress the jests of the casual visitor on noticing some of the more exotic attempts of the Flower Guild at Harvest Festival decoration. On the other hand, if the same person, week after week, persisted in unwelcome wit at the expense of the Flower Guild, attempts to quell him would sooner or later not be confined to mere stares. If the same norm is persistently violated by the same person, the retribution grows accordingly; furthermore, if the same person violates a large number of different norms, the punishment for the violation of each is likely to be greater than if he violated one alone.

Nevertheless, the sanctions which support the folkways of a society are a great deal less severe than those which support its mores, since these are believed to be essential for social welfare to a degree which folkways are not. Ordinarily, the mores are taken for granted as being a highly important part of the nature of things. It is only when the mores are called into question that people reflect on them. 'Belief rationalizes them in the form of myth, ritual expresses them in the form of symbols, and action embodies them in the form of right conduct.'[3] The mores are morally right, their violation morally wrong. The mores have no need of justification, because they exist in their own right. They are not subject to deliberate change or to analysis, and criticism of them draws strong punishment down on the head of the critic. There is a sense of unreflecting solidarity among people who share the same mores because their sentiments are alike; and there is a sense of resistance and antagonism towards anyone with different mores. Whereas foreign folkways are merely

21

disconcerting because they upset old habits and familiar grooves, foreign mores are deeply disturbing because, in addition, they offend profound sentiments.

Some mores refer to a relationship between two persons in a given relationship. There are strict moral rules for the behaviour of doctor and patient, or priest and confessor. Others are more general in character, such as the admonition to be honest, chaste or industrious. Thus we have not only specific mores requiring behaviour of a particular kind, but also general ones saying that whatever the specific rule, it should be obeyed. In this way, the mores try to guarantee their own enforcement.

But, of course, they do not always succeed in doing so and when mores come to have some special organization for their enforcement, then they are regarded as being laws. Seldom are all the mores thus enforced, only the more important ones. Since, however, there is no legislative body for the enactment of new rules not previously part of the cultural heritage, the law in this case should be called customary law. This category then includes everything between folkways and fully-developed law. In so far as human societies have had any law at all, this is what they have generally had. Only with the development of large-scale political organization, extensive specialization, and writing has complete or formal law come into existence. Enacted law is a more deliberate, more clearly stated, thing than folkways or mores. It is a product of conscious thought and planning, of deliberate formulation and voluntary application. It is not only necessitated by a complex society, but it also makes such a society possible. The things that are enacted into law usually begin as mores: so that the law is sometimes defined as 'mores given the specific sanction of governmental enforcement'. Laws which are not supported by folkways and mores usually have little chance of enforcement—a fact very clearly seen by the leaders of contemporary student protest movements. Yet superficial as they are from this point of view, laws perform a genuine function in giving precision, scope, and a means of enforcement to the mores in societies where multiplicity of groups and interests, accumulation of culture and improved means of communication have broken down the solidarity of the small community and substituted for it a larger, more dynamic and more secularized society.

Perhaps, after this rather lengthy disquisition on the nature and function of the principal groups of norms between which sociologists distinguish, we may now think a little more intelligently about the relationship of these groups of norms to social institutions themselves. So far, we have discussed social norms in terms of broad categories and only occasionally commented on the interdependence of these categories. In fact, folkways, mores and laws tend to be related in a systematic fashion, forming interwoven and clearly observable patterns of social control relating to the more important aspects of human behaviour. It is to these interwoven, often highly complicated patterns of 'expected' social behaviour that we give the name 'social institution'.

'An institution can be defined as a set of interwoven folkways, mores and laws built round one or more functions. It is a part of the social structure, set off by the closeness of its organization and by the distinctiveness of its functions.' Hence, Kingsley Davis argues, it is inclusive rather than exclusive of the concepts of folkways, mores and law, for without them, there could be no institutions:

Marriage, for example, embraces the complex of folkways surrounding the approved mating of men and women, including in our culture engagement and wedding rings, rice throwing, the honeymoon, lifting the bride over the threshold etc. etc. It also embraces certain mores—pre-marital chastity, postmarital fidelity, taking of the vows, obligation of support etc. Finally it embraces certain laws—record, right of divorce for cause, protection against fraud, proper age, absence of prohibitive kinship bonds etc. All these norms taken together form a definite structure, the institution of marriage, which has a meaning as a whole and which, when operative in behaviour, results in the performance of certain social and individual functions such as reproduction and child-rearing on the social side, sexual gratification and affection on the individual side. Similarly it can be said that economic, political, and religious institutions each represent a distinguishable set of interrelated folk-ways, mores and laws.[4]

The immense importance of these normative 'sets' to the sociologist should be immediately apparent. The quickest way to envisage the total social order of a society is to understand its major institutions and the relations between these institutions. If a person can grasp economic, political, religious and familial complexes of a society and can see how they are mutually interdependent, then he can grasp the most salient features of its entire social system. The rest is simply a matter of filling in. Often the specialist deals with only one institutional complex, such as the family, ignoring the rest, and this approach at least has the advantage of narrowing down the amount of material to be dealt with and makes it possible to relate social facts to social theory in a way which other types of specialists, notably social philosophers, have not always succeeded in doing satisfactorily. On the other hand, the need for a less myopic investigation of social institutions remains and is indeed essential for the development of a general rather than a segmental theory of social action. The nature of the inter-relationships of social institutions has long been a subject of sociological discussion. Marx, for example, underlined the peculiar relevance of economic institutions to the structure of other social institutions. Subsequently, Weber attempted to modify some of Marx's conclusions. More recent sociologists have been concerned to point out that on the inter-relationship between institutions depends the character of the whole society in which they operate:

The inter-relationship of the various institutions can be likened to a *wheel,* a unity of interdependence in structure and function. The family, which is at the centre and is the first institution the individual meets, is the *hub.* The *spokes* might be the education, religion, government and economic institutions. The *rim* would be the community within which the various institutions operate. Subordinate institutions connect and interconnect within and between the five named institutions.

As with all generalizations, there are a number of ways in which this particular one might be criticized and profitably modified. Above all, it should be said that the imagery on which it rests inevitably conveys a static relationship between the major institutions (after all, wheels are not usually constructed in such a way as to allow the spokes to vary in strength or in their relationship to each other, from time to time): nor does this particular model allow for the fact that though the 'rim' may remain in some ways unaltered, for example in its political limits, the 'spokes', and indeed the hub itself, can, and do, change both in structure and in function with the passage of time. The analogy of the wheel, that is to say, is an analogy which makes no concession to the concept of social change or to the related problems of the ways in which, and the reasons why, social institutions change, and in changing alter the character of the community in which they exist.

Tracing the development of individual social institutions used to be a full-time activity for the academic sociologist. Traditionally, in England as elsewhere, the study of the family, of religion, of law and social stratification was a quest for origins. Has the institution of the family always existed in human society? Was there a time when religion and religious institutions emerged, displacing previous systems of belief related to the supernatural, such as magic? Was there a time when man lived in a state of primitive democracy; when 'the happy savage' naturally and spontaneously so conducted himself as to make restraining codes of law unnecessary? Sociologists used to pose such questions as: 'Was the structure of the human family originally matriarchal or patriarchal in structure?', questions which, during a period when social Darwinism dominated such fields of intellectual enquiry, seemed of pressing academic interest. These questions about the origin and development of the human family required the use of historical documents, folklore and myth. To the extent that families were studied directly, they were

25

c

studied in broad compass only in the most 'primitive' societies. The assumption being that the family structure of these societies was similar to early forms of the human family, and that a study of such families would shed light on the origin and development of the human family. The contemporary family, like the rest of society, was assumed to be the culmination of the long evolutionary process, and not in need of direct study. (One should add in parenthesis that even had the need been felt, there would have been strong social and moral pressures to inhibit its satisfaction. The hammer of the geologist might indeed have cracked the Rock of Ages, but it had not yet broken down the door of the Englishman's home.) The results of these investigations carried out under the influence of social Darwinism were inconclusive and inconsistent. Morgan and Engels uncovered examples of 'promiscuity' and 'group marriage' in primitive society, while Westermarck produced evidence to show that primitive and even ape families were monogamous and faithful. This last contribution sparked off a whole series of investigations into the private lives of the higher primates, which have continued to the present day, and appear in some of the most recent symposia on the family under such titles as *A Field Study of the Behaviour and Social Relations of the Gibbon* and *Social Deprivation in Monkeys*. Equally inconclusive were attempts to prove that matriarchy was the prior form of family organization. While Sir Henry Maine amassed evidence to show that patriarchy was found in early forms of the family, Bachofen and Briffault produced evidence that matriarchy preceded patriarchy. Because the evidence was never clear-cut, and both sides could find data to support their ideology, the issues were never decided and, in the end, the attempt to discover the origins and the course of evolution of the family was abandoned as an unprofitable subject for investigation.

The discrediting of the evolutionary approach to the study of the family, as of the sociological investigation of other social institutions, inhibited further attempts to investigate the historical development of particular family forms for many years. Instead sociologists chose to study the family in contemporary societies emphasizing the importance of one particular form, the individual nuclear family, as a universal social phenomenon.

> It does not matter whether marital relations are permanent or temporary, whether there is polygyny or polyandry or sexual licence; whether conditions are complicated by the addition of members not included in *our* family circle; the one fact stands out beyond all others that everywhere the husband, wife and immature children constitute a unit apart from the remainder of the community.[5]

The universality of the nuclear family can be accounted for by the indispensable functions it performs and the difficulty of ensuring the performance of these functions by any other social group:

> In the nuclear family or its constituent relationships we thus see assembled four functions fundamental to human social life—the sexual, the economic, the reproductive, and the educational. . . . In addition, the family frequently, but not universally, draws to itself various other functions. Thus, it is often the center of religious worship with the father as family priest. It may be the primary unit in landholding, vengeance or recreation. Social status may depend more upon family position than upon individual achievement. And so on.[6]

The basic structure of the nuclear family depends upon incest taboos; from these it follows that the nuclear family is discontinuous over time and confined to two generations. A third generation can only result from the formation of new families by the exchange of males and females between existing nuclear families. In consequence, every normal adult in every human society belongs to at least two nuclear families —a family of orientation in which he was born and reared, and which includes his father, mother, brothers and sisters, and a family of procreation which he establishes by his own marriage and which includes his husband or wife, his sons and his daughters. The incest taboos and their extension outside the family, together with rules of descent, are the

27

source of all the complexities of kinship usages and terminology. The extended incest taboos establish interdependence between families and within families and thus play an important part in the integration of simple and peasant communities.

The universality of the nuclear family does not mean that family structure is everywhere the same. On the contrary, it is extremely variable. Some of the major items of variation are the number of spouses, authority, strength of bond, choice of spouse, residence and differences in the parent-child relation and in sibling relations. It is possible, however, to make a broad distinction between the family systems in which the nuclear family is relatively independent, and the systems in which the nuclear family is incorporated in, or subordinated to, a larger group, the polygamous or extended family.

The more or less independent nuclear family is characteristic of modern industrial societies. Its predominance seems to be due to the growth of individualism, reflected in property, law and general social ideals of individual happiness and self-fulfilment, and to geographical and social mobility. It has also been affected by the increasing state provision for individual misfortune; the individual is no longer largely or entirely dependent upon his family in times of stress, hence in large measure the solidarity and stability of this form of family depends on the quality rather than the profitability of the personal relationships between husband and wife, parents and children. Inevitably, the solidarity of the individual nuclear family is greater where it includes young, dependent children, but as the children grow up the bonds tend to weaken, first through the influence of peer groups, and later as a result of social and geographical mobility.

The composite forms of family are to be found frequently in preliterate or simple societies and also in many non-industrial societies. In Europe, forms of the extended family, for example the Yugoslav Zadruga, survived until the beginning of the present century. Different types of extended family are still common in Asia, even in an industrialized country such as Japan.

28

In all forms of family, the matter of crucial importance from the point of view of any individual member is the identification of the kin which together make up the effective family group. For readers in whose personal culture kinship is associated and indeed commonly identified with ties of blood, it is essential to recognize that this is neither necessarily nor universally the case. Kinship relationships are based on socially recognized and accepted roles defined in genealogical terms, not on biologically determined links. Hence, by adoption, one may become the son or daughter of parents to whom one has no relationship by blood whatsoever; and illegitimate children are sometimes referred to as 'having no father'. Social anthropologists have devoted much of their efforts to analysing the kinship systems of particular societies, and to the comparative study of kinship. Their interest reflects the fact that kinship is supremely important in primitive societies. It is a chief factor in maintaining social unity, and it constitutes the framework within which the individual is assigned economic and social functions, acquires rights and obligations, receives community aid, etc. Usually, therefore, the most effective way to study the social structure of a primitive society is, to begin with, the analysis of kinship. Sociologists, however, turning to the study of their own and neighbouring societies, have made a good deal less of the importance of kinship to the maintenance of social structure since they have readily, and not without the acquiescence of historians, assumed that kinship plays a far smaller part in the life of industrial societies which they have mainly studied. It is now clear, however, that they have done so to the detriment of a full understanding of the structure of such societies and of the family forms which exist within them. In the industrial working class, the class which has been most affected by the shifts and changes in the economy, it has been shown in a number of studies conducted during the last ten or fifteen years that kinship is still important in controlling individual behaviour and as a system of mutual aid. Indeed, it has been claimed that in this country, were it not for a well understood and accepted obligation on the part of the young to supply material and financial support for their elderly and ageing kinsfolk, the effective cost of our medical and social services to the old would be an incalculably greater burden that it already is. Further, it is quite clear from such investigations as have been made that were grandmothers not so obviously prepared to help care for the children of young mothers out at work, the size of the female working population of this country would be significantly, and will be increasingly, depleted and the standard of living to which we have become accustomed thereby diminished. Nor is kinship and family structure without significance among higher-status groups. Very soon after the last war, a number of studies were made into social mobility: what factors affected the type of education children received; the relative success of working-class children in attaining occupations of high social status; the degree to which occupation of the father influenced the occupation of the son, etc. Whatever criticism may be levelled against aspects of the techniques adopted in some of these studies, together they are a substantial and convincing testimony to the influence of family on the ultimate status of their individual younger members. Working-class children continue to be relatively under-represented in the higher professions and in the governing élite not because they are necessarily less able than middle- and upper-class children, but because the homes in which they themselves are brought up provide less stimulus and fewer social contacts which might stimulate an interest in and acquisition of those skills which are associated in contemporary society with the entry to high-status occupations. Children are not 'born' doctors, lawyers or teachers, but they are born into the households of doctors, lawyers and teachers and tend to enter these or similar occupations themselves, partly because of parental ambition, but not least because it is simpler and easier in a variety of ways to choose the familiar rather than the unfamiliar.

That family should continue to exert an undeniable influence on the ultimate achievement of the younger is undoubtedly a matter of some concern to politicians, not least in societies where social mobility, equality of opportunity and individual achievement are regarded as both desirable and necessary. To the sociologist, who has long held that the family is the basic unit of social organization, this can be but a confirmation of a basic premise. Not all politicians, however, have been content to leave sociological assumptions unchallenged. Any who are familiar with the history of the early years of the U.S.S.R. will recall that it was the avowed intention of some of the most prominent of the Bolshevik leaders that the family should cease to function as the socializing agency of children: '... the contemporary family ... has no productive functions and to leave all care for posterity to this private collection cannot be justified by any positive considerations....' For one reason or another, participants in the debates of those years agreed that fathers and mothers did more harm than good, and that, in a society organized around a collective work system, it was more appropriate to accustom a child from the earliest years to life in a collective of peers rather than training him in the individualistic family.

In the event it proved more difficult than some of the early prophets of the Revolution had imagined to set aside the natural ties of affection between parents and children, and to undermine the authority and responsibility of the family unit. More significantly, however, it seemed that where this had to some extent been achieved, certain pathological situations had arisen in the community which were a social embarrassment internally and a potential source of external criticism of the viability of the socialist system. It seems, for example, that where parents had indeed abrogated their authority over their children, the state had failed to provide adequate or effective substitute institutions for the orientation and socialization of children, with the result that vagrancy, crime and delinquency were becoming increasingly worrying social problems. Within less than twenty years, therefore, Soviet propaganda swung away from its original policy of denouncing family as an obstacle to the realization of socialist hopes and turned its full approval on the family as a social institution.

To achieve the desired effect, the Soviets proceeded radically to restate their views on the nature of marriage and its responsibilities. Whereas in the early, heroic, days of the Revolution, marriage had been politically and legally represented as largely if not entirely, a matter for the individuals concerned, from the mid-1930s marriage was increasingly represented in legislation as permanent, lifelong union of so much concern to the state that only the children of such unions as had been registered with the authorities had the right to claim the name or the estate of their biological father, From 1944, only registered marriages were recognized as legally binding and conferring social and economic rights.

From Russian experience, it would thus appear that the individual family is a unit of such resilience that it can, and does, survive the most determined attempts both to undermine its authority and to substitute other institutions to perform its basic functions. Close analysis of the outcome of a very different kind of experiment to achieve a similar affect, the Israeli Kibbutz, only serves to underline just how true this is.

It is worthwhile noticing that, despite the well-worn sociological aphorism that 'marriage is rooted in the family, not the family in marriage', it is commonly the case, as in Russia, that it is changes in the regulations surrounding marriage that are popularly believed to affect the stability of the family. Hence, when in the U.S.S.R. the strengthening of the family was urged upon the populace as one of the basic rules of communist morality, the authorities proceeded to enforce this view by introducing legislation which not only emphasized the importance of the public regulation of marriage, but also increasingly determined (and delimited) the circumstances under which marriages might be set aside. So that the alleged sexual frivolity, child neglect and juvenile delinquency which had stemmed from the early, permissive, view of marriage might be halted, *Pravda* declared that 'marriage is the most serious affair in life', and published long articles extolling the virtues of the more stringent marriage laws.

The actual relationship between marriage regulation in general, and divorce laws in particular, to the stability of the family as a social institution is a good deal less clear than may at first sight appear from the arguments and the advantages claimed for mere statutory manipulation. All societies have regulations, some more elaborate than others, regarding the conditions under which a valid marriage may be contracted. Since all societies need to ensure both the efficient rearing of the young of a species amongst whom dependence on parental support is prolonged and the establishment of legitimate lines of descent through which claims to name, property, status, etc., can be clearly established, sanctions are provided to uphold and maintain a particularly stable relationship between men and women in which these ends may be accomplished. Hence, whatever the degree of freedom of choice of marriage partner a society may allow, all societies impose clear restrictions on the circumstances in which valid marriages may be set aside, lest unlimited freedom here inhibit the adequate fulfilment of the basic family task. It is precisely because stability of marriage is supposed to guarantee stability of family structure that so much attention has been paid to the fluctuation in the rates at which marriages are set aside in individual societies, particularly in those, such as our own, where the divorce rate has risen significantly over the past three decades. There is, however, little to suggest a correlation between so-called 'liberal' divorce laws and a high prevailing divorce rate. There is, on the other hand, much to suggest that family form and divorce rate are connected in so far as societies in which the nuclear family is set in and supported by some form of composite family structure tend to have fewer divorces than societies such as our own and the United States of America, where the independent, nuclear family is highly developed.

Family form, and the sanctions on which it rests, as we have already briefly mentioned, is closely associated with economic structure, but it is also very much affected by other influences, not least religious influences. A familiar explanation of the increased rate at which valid marriages are set aside in contemporary societies, both in the West and elsewhere, and of the instability of the family which it is said to reveal, is that this is the result of the secularization of society and

33

the rejection of the authority of religious bodies which traditionally were held to be authoritative. While changes in economic institutions have been a major factor in bringing about changes in the family, the influence of religion has usually been to preserve established forms of the family. The extent to which societies are, or have become, secularized is at the moment perhaps more a matter of debate than actual, detailed knowledge, but it is increasingly true that, whereas religious sanctions were acknowledged as having general authority in pre-industrial societies, now religious sanctions are held only to be relevant for the decreasing number of religious adherents. Religious leaders themselves are more inclined to share this view than oppose it, arguing that it is both impossible and improper to attempt to embody in legislation an ideology which the larger number of people regard as irrelevant to their lives.

Be this as it may, it is of some considerable importance to notice that in a good many so-called 'secular societies' a prominence is given to the views and advice of religious leaders, even when they are neither shared nor ultimately accepted, which many political leaders might well envy. The continued social significance of the religious leader, together with the remarkable growth of certain types of religious organization in advanced industrial societies (neither of which fit easily into some of the earlier predictions of sociologists) has given an added impetus to the sociological study of religion during the past decade, and given a distinctive focus to the studies which have been conducted.

The early sociological studies of religion had three distinctive methodological characteristics: they were evolutionist, positivist and psychologistic. These features may well be illustrated from the work of Comte, Tylor and Spencer. In Comte's sociology, one of the fundamental conceptions is the so-called 'Law of the Three Stages', according to which human thought has passed historically and necessarily, from the theological through the metaphysical to the positive stage. Comte treated theological thinking as intellectual error, which is dispersed by the rise of modern science. He traced within the theological stage a development from animism to monotheism; and he explained religious belief in psychological terms by reference to the thought processes and perceptions of early man.

The work of Sir E. B. Tylor, *Primitive Culture*, 1871, and Herbert Spencer, *Principles of Sociology*, Vol. III, 1896, was more rigorous and shows more clearly the features we have mentioned above. Both thinkers were concerned to explain, in the first place, the origin of religion. They believed that the soul was the principal feature of religious belief and set out to give an account in relationalistic terms of how such a belief might have originated in the mind of primitive man. According to this, man obtained his idea of the soul from the misinterpretation of dreams and death. As with Comte, their explanation of religious phenomena is in terms of religious dispositions, intellectual errors and the condition of social life. Other social scientists of the nineteenth century, notably Karl Marx and Sir J. G. Frazer, approached the study of religion in a similar way.

An alternative approach, however, was formulated by Émile Durkheim in *Les formes élémentaires de la vie réligieuse*, 1912, in which he argued that in all societies a distinction is made between the *sacred* and the *profane*. Religion, he asserted, is 'a unified system of beliefs and practices relative to sacred things, that is things set apart and forbidden—beliefs and practices which unite into a single community called a Church all those who adhere to them'. In Durkheim's theory, the collective aspects of religion are emphasized: the function of religious rituals is to affirm the moral superiority of the society over its individual members and thus to maintain the solidarity of the group. 'The god of the clan can be nothing but the clan itself.'

Durkheim's emphasis on ritual as against belief was to prompt later anthropologists to undertake functional investigations of religion. The work of B. Malinowski in *Magic Science and Religion*, 1925, and of A. R. Radcliffe-Brown in *The Andaman Islanders*, 1922, has shown how religion works in simple societies to maintain and to control individual conduct.

In the study of civilized societies, however, Durkheim's

theory has proved less helpful, for here religion has frequently been as divisive as it is unifying. That is to say, while it unites particular groups it may provoke conflict between groups of the larger society. Moreover, in civilized societies and especially in modern societies, beliefs and doctrines are of more importance than ritual. In the result, therefore, the sociological study of religion has diverged from that of anthropology and has been characterized in a number of ways. L. T. Hobhouse, for example, was largely concerned with the influence of intellectual development on moral ideas. Hence, in discussing religion in his major work, *Morals in Evolution*, 1906, he is entirely concerned with the moral codes of the major religions and especially Christianity. The codes are examined as doctrines and analysed in largely philosophical terms. Their relation to social behaviour is considered in very general terms.

Max Weber's treatment of religious belief, however, differs in several important respects. In the first place, it is not based on an evolutionary scheme. Secondly, it is largely concerned with a single major aspect of religious ethics, namely the connection with the economic order, which he examines from two points of view. First, the influence of particular religious doctrines upon economic behaviour; second, the relations between the position of groups in the economic order and types of religious beliefs. Moreover, Weber is less concerned with the ethical doctrines as expounded by theologians than with these doctrines in their popular form as the guide to everyday behaviour. Weber's best known work, *The Protestant Ethic and the Spirit of Capitalism* (trans. 1930), which was the starting point for his studies of religion, aims to show the part played in the origin and development of modern capitalism by Calvinist ethics.

Since the work of Weber and Durkheim, few theoretical contributions have been made to the sociological study of religion. Weber's own work has stimulated two principal and related lines of enquiry; one concerning the characteristics, doctrines, and social significance of religious sects, and the other dealing with the connection between social classes and religious sects. In this field, an important contribution came from his friend, Ernst Troeltsch, whose *Social Teaching of the Christian Churches,* 1911, gave a more detailed account than Weber's of the social ethics of different Christian churches and sects. In the same field of concern with sectarian movements is H. R. Niebuhr's *The Social Sources of Denominationalism,* 1929. More recently, there have been detailed empirical studies of particular sects in terms of their relations and responses to the social milieu in which they exist, of which, in this country, perhaps the best known is Bryan Wilson's *Sects and Society,* 1961.

From what has been said so far, it will have become manifestly apparent that, although both sociologists and theologians are interested in the study of religion, they are not basically interested either in the same things or in the same data. Sociologists are not concerned to engage in the critical analysis of the source, structure and validity of religious texts; they are concerned to see whether the use and acceptance of such texts affect overt social behaviour. They are not directly concerned to trace the development and acceptance of religious concepts; they are committed to investigating whether or not the acceptance of new religious concepts is associated with the emergence of new social groupings or the restructuring of existing ones, and whether the new or restructured religious groups engage in different types of social activity and expression than foregoing ones. Perhaps it would not be entirely misleading to say that, whilst theologians are concerned with the Faith, sociologists are largely interested in the activities of the faithful. On the other hand, it must be admitted that sociologists have sometimes fallen into the error of believing that it is possible to pursue the study of the one in complete ignorance of the other. Where this has been the case, their sins have surely found them out, as criticisms of their work by professional theologians have only too clearly demonstrated, not least in the case of Weber himself.

In passing, it is interesting to notice that although theologians may, from time to time, criticize the sociological study of religion on intellectual grounds, they do not oppose it on moral grounds. There has been nothing comparable to the

37

bitterness which once existed between Church spokesman and the early Freudian students of religion. The explanation of this contrast rests on a number of factors, not least that the climate of intellectual enquiry is no longer dominated by traditional embargoes on the scientific exploration of particular subjects of which religion was certainly one. Even so, this can be only a partial explanation, since the period when a good deal of the early work of the direct study of institutions by sociologists was undertaken pre-dates or overlaps the time of the squabbles between the Freudians and the theologians. The significant difference between the work of people such as Tylor and Marrett and that of Freud, however, is that the sociologists sought to explain, not explain away, religious observance. Moreover, their assumption that religion was a necessary social phenomena and their implication that the monotheistic religion of their contemporaries represents the highest, most sophisticated, form of religion achieved by man was less likely to affront religious opinion than Freud's account of religion as a survival of beliefs and experiences of the most primitive kind. Perhaps the next generation of sociologists, many of whose personal views were a good deal more cynical, might have precipitated a clash with religious opinion had they chosen to pursue the study of religion. In fact, regarding it as an institution of diminishing influence and more concerned to explain the urgent problems of poverty, crime and social inequality, the majority of them chose to write on other subjects. Those who continued to work in the field of the sociology of religion were largely concerned to draw attention to the importance of religion to mankind as a source of personal and social stability. Charles H. Cooley, for example, wrote that

. . . human beings are like a party of men with lanterns making their way through an immeasurable forest. To all except the intellectually blasé or the stupid, the perplexities of life sooner or later are considered as being too great for man to meet out of his own resources. Herein lies the permanency of religious attitudes and groups.[7]

More recent studies, especially those concerned with the small religious sects, have taken a less cosmic view of religious expression and have attempted to relate religious affiliation to immediate social environment. Nevertheless, it is clear that they are evidence of a continuing and, indeed, increasing interest in religion as the object of serious sociological investigation.

There are, of course, disadvantages in concentrating attention on the structure and activities of the small religious sects, to which only a minority of religious adherents belong, for it leaves virtually unanswered the question as to how and in what respects practising membership of a particular religion influences individual or group behaviour in the wider society. Superficially, where the religious and the political society are one, this particular problem may appear not to be particularly complicated, but in contemporary Western societies, where only a minority of the total population are religious adherents, it quite clearly is. Furthermore, Weber's work on Protestantism is an indication of how even more difficult it is to satisfy curiosity on this point when one recalls that one denomination may have a very different social influence than another denomination of the same faith. This last point, however, does not commonly appear to interest the majority of the public when asked their opinion on matters relating to the influence of religion in contemporary society. In England, for example, a number of national surveys have been conducted in the past few years into the attitude of parents to the present statutory requirement for religious education in state schools. Less than one in ten of those whose opinions were invited wished such a requirement to be dropped in future legislation. The reason that was given by the majority was that 'it teaches children the difference between good and bad, between right and wrong'. Whether moral codes actually need religious sanctions to be effective is a profoundly important sociological question. Certainly, humanists do not subscribe to such a view and in the course of its history, Christianity, the religion in which these parents wish to have their children instructed, has not invariably been concerned with morality. In contrast to

Judaism, there have been times when Christianity has in fact obscured the problem of morality in the search for individual salvation.

Sociological studies of morality and its association with religious systems are, however, disappointingly few and very limited in scope. In the United States, there have been David Riesman's *The Lonely Crowd*, 1950, and W. H. Whyte's *The Organization Man*, 1957, both of which are concerned with the decline of the Protestant ethic in American society, but also indicate some more general features of morality in modern societies, above all the separation between religion and morality. But just how far this separation has gone in individual societies and to what degree English parents, who for the most part do not attend a church, are deluding themselves that the moral structures of their society are in some way inextricably bound up with the religious education of their children we do not know.

On the other hand, we certainly do know that in modern industrial societies, whatever the real or imaginary relevance of religious sanctions to the maintenance of moral structure, they are considered wholly irrelevant to another institutional aspect of such societies, the way in which they are divided up into classes or strata which form a hierarchy of prestige and power. There are societies, both past and present, in which the stratified system is connected with religious beliefs. Both systems of estates and caste systems are reinforced by and make direct appeal to religious sanctions to maintain and explain their respective hierarchies, with the result that they are inevitably weakened by the advent of modern industrialism, which emphasizes both rationality and the importance of material reward for individual effort and excellence.

Most highly developed in India, the caste system, with its four traditional castes, the Brahman, Kshatriya, the Vaisya and the Sudra, and myriad sub-castes, is directly related to the *varna* system as expounded in the ancient religious literature of India. M. N. Srinivas observed in *Religion and Society among the Coorgs of South India,* 1966, that the notions of *karma,* which 'teach a Hindu that he is born in a particular sub-caste because he deserved to be born there', and *dharma,* the code of duties (or rules of the caste), 'have contributed very greatly to the idea of hierarchy which is inherent in the caste system'. The concept of pollution, he says, is 'fundamental to the caste system and every type of caste relation is governed by it'.

That the caste system is reinforced by religious sanctions does not, of course, exclude the fact that it is also evidently connected with economic differentiation, as are all other forms of social stratification. E. Senart, in a classical study, *Caste in India,* 1894, observes that the *varnas* are themselves related to hierarchically arranged occupational groups. Thus the Brahmans are priests; the Kshatriya nobles and warriors; the Vaisya traders, farmers and money-lenders and the Sudra serfs and manual labourers. It is precisely this hierarchical ordering of society, based on broad divisions of labour which were regarded as having definite functions, that prompts Senart to argue that the *varnas* originally resembled feudal estates. Resembled, but were not identical with, since the religious system with which *varnas* are associated was vastly different from Christianity, the religious system which, in the West, reinforced feudal estate systems. In both systems, the rewards for this life were to be found in the next; but whilst Hindus believed this to be the next life on Earth, Christians looked for their reward in Heaven.

The feudal estates of medieval Europe had three important characteristics. First, as we have already mentioned, they were associated with divisions of labour. 'The nobility were ordained to defend all, the clergy to pray for all, and the commons to provide food for all.'

Second, they were legally defined; each estate had a status in the precise sense of a legal complex of rights and duties, of privileges and obligations. Thus, as has been said, to know a person's real position it was first of all necessary to know 'the law by which he lived'. In the twelfth century, when serfdom was increasing and a legal theory of the feudal estate was emerging, the English lawyer Glanville listed the disabilities of serfs as being: inability to appeal to the king for justice; absence of rights over their chattels and holdings; liability to pay the fines of *merchet* and *heriot.*

41

The differences between estates can be seen also in the different penalties imposed for similar offences.

Third, the feudal estates were political groups. Stubbs, in his *Constitutional History of England*, 1878, wrote: 'An assembly of estates is an organized collection ... of several orders, estates or conditions of men who are recognized as possessing political power.' In this sense, the serfs did not constitute an estate. Indeed, classical feudalism knew only two estates, the nobility and the clergy. The decline of European feudalism after the twelfth century is associated with the rise of a third estate, not the serfs or villeins, but of the burghers, who as Henri Pirenne points out, behaved for a long period as a distinctive group within the feudal system before they overthrew it.

The actual system of feudal estates was more complex, more varied and less rigid than this brief account can show. The distinctions within estates and the political aspects of feudalism are fully and accurately discussed in Marc Bloch's *La Société féodale*, 1940, where the concept of *fief*, on which relations within and between estates depended, is also discussed admirably.

To accept the grant of rights and title to a fief (usually land, although it could be any desirable thing, such as an office, revenue in money or kind, the right to collect tolls, etc.) was to become the vassal of the benefactor, to whom were given in return pledges of loyalty and services, the faithful performance of which guaranteed the continued right to the fief. The obligations of the vassal were not primarily intended to be economic, but political and moral. Hence the obligations of military service and court service, the duty both to help the lord to form a court and to submit to the judgments of the lord's court and none other.

In addition to these two sets of obligations there was a third, made up of financial obligations to the lord, of which 'relief', the sum paid by a vassal's heir for the lord's recognition of his father's fief, was of critical importance. Although a son might inherit his father's fief, he inherited the rights of tenancy, not of ownership. Every holder of a fief was a tenant of one higher than himself. Hence one man's lord was another man's vassal. Not until the highest were reached was there any conception of 'ownership', and even then the most exalted were seen as owing obedience to one higher than themselves: God.

Where social stratification is based on a legally defined system of specific rights and obligations, with a peculiar emphasis on the latter in the light of contemporary teleology, both the opportunity and the desire for individual self-aggrandisement are inhibited to a degree unknown in our own immediate society. Systems of estates, like caste systems, are the product of societies where it is counted as a virtue to a man that he serves faithfully in that station into which he was born and to which Providence or *karma* has assigned a particular and essential function.

By contrast, industrial capitalist societies not only require but positively stimulate personal initiative and individual ambition as a means of maintaining and increasing their efficiency, their wealth and their power. The system of social stratification in such societies has thus to be a good deal more open, more flexible and independent of sanctions which operate to uphold the *status quo ante* and social distinctions which appeal to tradition, the law and to Providence or *karma*. Such systems of social stratification are described as *class* systems.

So familiar are we today with the term *social class* that the vagueness of its meaning to sociologists and to politicians, both of whom make constant use of it, tends to escape unnoticed. Considerable difficulties do, in fact, arise when the attempt is made to specify the number of social classes, or to define their membership precisely. That such difficulties are not immediately perceived is a consequence of some of the assumptions on which a number of empirical studies of social class have been based, either not being made explicit, or not being examined critically either by those undertaking them or by those who read the results. One well-known study of the composition of social classes in England, conducted after the last war, purported to show that occupation was the effective index of class and that, if one could ascertain a man's occupation, it was a relatively simple matter to allocate him to a particular social class. Despite the immediate attraction of so simple a research tool, its precision is undoubtedly diminished when one scrutinizes the research methods on which the original study was based. Informants, who in this case were drawn from groups who are far from typical of the community at large, were in fact limited in the freedom with which they were allowed to rank the various occupations specified. In particular, they were asked to place occupations within a simple three-tier, hierarchically arranged system of social stratification. Whatever else may be said of this feature of the investigation, it certainly implies not merely that there is general agreement about the effective number of classes which exist in English society and that the divisions between them are clearly perceived, but also that the internal differences between social classes are greater and of more significance than the differences within them. None of these propositions could be adequately sustained by such sociological information as we have at present, which on the contrary seems to indicate how dubious each of them really is. In fact, the divisions between classes are so imprecise as to have eluded sociological analysis, and sociologists have contented themselves with making studies of individual social classes whose reality is assumed and whose limits are left undisclosed. Furthermore, the internal cohesiveness of social classes, their role in society and their future is the focus for a good deal of disagreement among sociologists. This becomes especially noticeable in studies of the so-called middle class which has been more the subject of investigation than any other.

On the working class, the classical study is that of G. Briefs, *The Proletariat,* 1938, which begins from a Marxist definition and expands it to introduce a discussion of the relation of the working classes to the white-collar middle class. General studies of the middle class include C. Wright Mills, *White Collar,* 1951, and Lewis and Maude, *The English Middle Classes,* 1953; but there have been many accounts of specific groups within the middle classes, and especially of the liberal professions. It has proved less easy to study the upper classes, and most sociological writing here extends from theoretical and historical studies of élites to studies based upon statistical information about property ownership, lines of descent and inheritance and educational privilege. One of the more interesting of recent studies of the higher echelons of contemporary industrial societies is C. Wright Mills, *The Power Élite,* 1956.

It is of considerable importance to notice how the simple association of property and wealth with membership of a particular social class has been progressively qualified in such studies. Whereas in the early days of industrial capitalism these factors appeared to be of paramount importance, in the twentieth century they appear to have become of less significance. So much so, that Carr-Saunders and Caradog Jones, writing in the early 1930s, went so far as to assert that social class had become an almost meaningless concept since they found it impossible to discern any 'natural breaks' in the foreshortened, levelling-out graphs of income and wealth which they were able to draw at that time. Only by making economic distinctions of the most arbitrary kind, they claimed, was it possible to speak of a contemporary 'class-structure'. There is a sort of disingenuous charm about such a statement, especially when one now reflects on the nature and bitterness of the political conflicts of the nineteen-thirties. No present-day sociologist, however, would be disposed to argue for or against the reality of social classes in contemporary society exclusively on the basis of differences of real income or wealth, both of which have become increasingly affected by the imposition of progressive and sometimes punitive taxation. Despite the tremendous and far from spent influence of Marxist theory of social classes, which is essentially economic in character, it is now generally accepted that although the basis of social class is indisputably economic, social classes have always been more than economic groups, in the narrow sense of that term. Moreover, in contemporary society, it appears that it is how one earns one's money and spends it which is of greater importance to social ranking rather than simply the amount one earns.

The study of patterns of consumption has complicated the study of social stratification in industrial societies, since it has drawn attention to the existence of *status groups* as well as social classes. Max Weber was the first to distinguish rigorously between the two, and to examine their inter-relation. With some over-simplification one might say that 'classes' are stratified according to their relation to the pro-duction and acquisition of goods; whereas 'status groups' are stratified according to the principles of their *consumption* of goods as represented by special 'styles of life'. The notion of social status has been analysed by a number of writers, both here and in the United States. T. H. Marshall, in an essay on 'The Nature and Determinants of Social Status', examined the factors which produce differences in status, as well as different types of status—personal, positional, etc. Subse-quently, discussing the changes in social stratification in capi-talist societies, he argued that there has been a shift from class organization to status organization, or as he terms it, from multibonded but undimensional groups to multidimen-sional and unibonded groups.

There have been many empirical studies of status groups, especially in terms of occupational differentiation. Indeed, as in the study to which we have already made reference, many of the more recent investigations of social stratification have been carried out largely in terms of occupational prestige scales. The predominant influence of American soci-ology has been important in this field. In the U.S.A., which has no strong tradition of class organization or ideological conflict, sociologists have naturally been concerned with stratification in those aspects which characterize American society—status and mobility. Unfortunately, in stratification studies of other societies which do inherit a tradition of class organization, status has sometimes been confused with class.

Although such a confusion is unhelpful, it is to some extent understandable, particularly in the light of the obser-vations of Marshall and others on the increasing importance of status groups in Western social hierarchies. T. Bottomore argues, for example, that in Western societies :

the social hierarchy is now constituted less by social classes and more by status groups. The difference broadly is between a hierarchy of a small number of organized or partly organized economic groups whose relations to each other are antagonistic, and a hierarchy of numerous groups more directly described as aggregates of individuals of equal social prestige, based on similarities which are not exclusively economic, and whose relations to each other are not primarily antagonistic but are partly competitive and partly emulative.[8]

It has often been said that it is only useful to define a social group as a 'social class' if its members manifest in their behaviour and their attitudes an awareness of their membership of a group within which all share common interests which are radically different from and bring them into conflict with other similar groups higher or lower on the social scale. It is of some interest to notice two things about this sort of claim.

Firstly, it vastly oversimplifies the nature of class consciousness. In society man will often spontaneously recognize others 'like themselves' and choose to associate with them without 'consciously' or deliberately reflecting that they are 'their class'. In actual fact, the conscious recognition of social class is most frequently prompted by deliberately mounted propaganda, which both stresses the common identity and interest of a far larger group than that in which most men move— far larger than any of them are spontaneously aware—and also underlines the wider differences that exist between classes than within them. Class consciousness based on propaganda does not, of course, necessarily have to be artificial. It merely illustrates the well-known fact that large-scale common interests can only be understood by some effort of the imagination which most of us are unlikely to make without some stimulus—as the leaders of the early trade union movement learned to their cost.

Second and even more significant, is the stress placed on the element of conflict and antagonism inherent in class organization, since it draws attention to the essentially invidious nature of social ranking by classes which the competitive nature of industrial capitalism inevitably engenders.

Compared with systems of estates and castes, which teach the wisdom of contentment with one's lot, class organization, with its promise of social advancement and material reward for individual effort, plants the seed of discontent in the individual mind which it proceeds to nurture by the sophisticated device of prompting rational reflection on the potential of man in society whilst at the same time inhibiting the full exercise of this potential to a large number. In a competitive situation, some will win and some lose in this particular race; it seems not possible for all to run and all to receive a prize; certainly not prizes of equal worth. Yet all must contribute to the prize money.

On the other hand, it is certainly true that though rewards are not equal, they are clearly a good deal more equal than they were, for example, in pre-industrial English society.

This is especially true of economic rewards, the 'carrots' of the capitalist system. Recent sociological studies in property in industrial societies have been largely concerned with two aspects: first, the distribution of property and its social effects; and second, the separation of the ownership and control of industrial enterprises in modern capitalism. There have been numerous studies of the distribution of wealth and income. In Britain, one of the earliest and still one of the more interesting is R. H. Tawney's *Equality,* revised edition 1952, which examines in detail the inequalities of wealth and income and their connection with the class system. H. Dalton, in *The Inequality of Incomes,* 1920, showed that the unequal distribution of wealth is a principal factor in producing inequalities of income. For the U.S.A. there is a great deal of useful information on the distribution of wealth and income in C. Wright Mills, *The Power Élite,* 1956, to which Vance Packard's later studies of *The Status Seekers* and *The Pyramid Climbers* are a later, and lighter, addendum. These and other studies indicate that there has been a movement towards greater economic equality in many of the advanced industrial countries since the beginning of the twentieth century, though it has been more marked in respect of incomes than in respect of property. Nevertheless, the present typical form of private property in these societies, the single transferable share, has made the potential distribution of property ownership wider than the traditional property form of pre-industrial societies, land, could ever have been and thereby encouraged many more to participate in, not eschew, the capitalist economy. As Tawney sardonically remarks, 'men do not throw stones at the glass house they intend to inhabit themselves'.

Dispersion of ownership has been accompanied by the separation of ownership and control in industrial enterprises, a phenomenon which has attracted much attention from sociologists concerned with the development of modern capitalism. It has resulted from the extension of the joint stock principle in the marketing of company shares. The industrial capitalists of the early nineteenth century were both owners and managers of their enterprises. But as the enterprises grew larger, more and more capital had to be drawn from outside, and this was made possible by joint stock legislation which made legal, on a scale previously unknown, the issue of share stock for sale on the open market. At present, the large companies which dominate the major branches of industry are managed and directed by individuals who do not own them. The owners of most of the capital are the thousands of small and medium shareholders who have little interest except in the profitability of the company.

Although the managers of modern industry do not own the enterprises outright, they usually have an important holding, and are frequently wealthy men in their own right. Moreover, both in Britain and the U.S.A., a tiny minority of the thousands of shareholders of individual companies, in fact, between them hold a very substantial proportion of the shares, certainly enough to give this group control of the enterprise. Hence it is important to speak of separation, not divorce, of the ownership and control of industrial property and to note, *inter alia,* C. Wright Mills' comment in *The Power Élite*: 'the chief executives and the very rich are *not* two distinct and clearly segregated groups'.

The rapid growth of large-scale enterprise, and the concentration of economic power, can be seen in all the industrial countries, whether their property system is one of largely private ownership or of mixed public and private ownership or even of complete collective ownership. In the U.S.S.R., as in Britain and the U.S.A., a small number of individuals manage the giant enterprises upon which material well-being depends and decide the major economic issues as to the use of economic resources. In all cases they have great power, and it is increasingly difficult for the mass of the population to exercise control over their use of power. In those capitalist countries where some of the basic industries have been nationalized, problems have arisen in the control of the public corporations which manage them. From the point of view of the employee and the ordinary citizen, public bureaucracies may be no easier to deal with, and no more egalitarian or devoted to the common good, than private managements. In many communist countries, the cost of public bureaucracy has been painfully reckoned in recent years. Both these types of experience remind one of Weber's prediction, in 'Politics as a Vocation',[9] and in the future development of industrial society there was a distinct danger that socialism might result not in the liberation of man, but in his enslavement to an all-powerful bureaucracy.

Studies of the institution of property illustrate well the point we made at the outset, that social institutions are inextricably related to one another. A number of the early studies, inspired by an interest in the evolutionary development of property, attempted to distinguish the principal forms of property, or the actual stages of its development as an institution in human societies. Thus L. T. Hobhouse, in his contribution, 'The Historical Evolution of Property, in Fact and Idea', to Bishop Gore's *Property, its Duties and Rights*, 1913, develops a three-stage theory of its development: the first, in which there is little social differentiation, little inequality, and in which economic resources are owned in common or are strictly controlled by the community; the second, in which wealth increases, great inequalities appear, and individual or collective ownership escapes from community control; and a third in which a conscious attempt is made to diminish inequality, and to restore community

control. More recent writers have rejected, here as elsewhere, the notion of unilinear evolution of property, whilst
not abandoning an interest in the development of particular
forms.

They have emphasized to a greater degree than Hobhouse's theoretical framework allowed, the complexity of
the inter-relations between the property system, the organization of industry, social stratification, political organization
and ideological systems. They have also served to demonstrate an essential feature of the functions of the family in
human society, since these are shown to vary with the variations in other social institutions. Moreover, it is clear that
the *ways* in which the nuclear family performs its major
function of socializing the child are also determined by other
elements in society. The family first socializes the child, but
it does not originate the values which it imparts; these come
from religion, political ideology, caste or class. The specific
character of the nuclear family in any society is thus determined by other social institutions; it does not determine
them. Similarly, social change originates in other institutions,
not in the family: the family changes in response.

It is this complexity of inter-relations between social institutions which makes their study at the same time both
fascinating and formidable. It also makes it very difficult
to compare particular social institutions of one society with
those of another, since not only may superficial likenesses between societies often mask basic dissimilarities, but in complex societies such as our own it is a far from simple matter
to establish the ways and means by which social institutions operate in the heterogeneous groups which together
constitute the society. Understandably in a subject in which,
as the following chapters will reveal, there are many other
aspects which can command the interested study of sociologists, an increasing number of them have turned away
from the study of social institutions themselves, preferring to
concentrate on isolated problems relating to them. Hence the
diminishing number of studies of the family as a social
institution and the increasing proliferation of articles on
dating, mating and divorce. All of these are interesting in

themselves, but tend to leave us ignorant of the structure and the organization of the institution itself, to the detriment of our full understanding of the structure and organization of the society which it supports.

SUGGESTED READING

BELL, N. W., and VOGEL, E. F., *A Modern Introduction to the Family* (Glencoe Illinois: Free Press, third edition, 1967).

YINGER, J. M., *Religion, Society and the Individual* (New York: Macmillan, 1957).

SCHLATTER, R., *Private Property, The History of an Idea* (Allen and Unwin, 1952).

LASLETT, P., and RUNCIMAN, W., *Philosophy, Politics and Society* (Oxford: Basil Blackwell, third series, 1967).

NOTES

1 W. G. Sumner, *Folkways* (Boston: Ginn, 1906).
2 *Ibid.*
3 *Ibid.*
4 *Human Society* (New York: Macmillan, 1948).
5 R. H. Lowie, *Primitive Society* (Routledge & Kegan Paul, 1920), pp. 66–7.
6 G. P. Murdock, *Social Structure* (Macmillan, 1949).
7 C. H. Cooley, *Social Organization*, 1909, p. 107.
8 *Classes in Modern Society* (Allen & Unwin, 1955).
9 H. H. Gerth and C. W. Mills (translators), *From Max Weber: Essays in Sociology* (Routledge & Kegan Paul, 1948).

3

Social Organizations

Anne Crichton

Before the industrial revolution, most people lived in villages as they do today in the developing countries. The village was dominated by the landowner who rented some of his land to tenants. Together with the yeoman farmers the landowners provided work for the labouring families and enabled them to earn a living. A description of life in one of the East Anglian landowning families is to be found in the fifteenth- and sixteenth-century Paston letters referred to by G. M. Trevelyan in his *English Social History* :

> When once a lady was married, she entered on a sphere of activity, influence and even authority. The Paston letters tell the tale of several generations of matrons by no means slaves to their husbands, but rather their counsellors and trusted lieutenants. They seem utterly devoted to their lords' interests, to which their numerous children must be sacrificed. They are better wives and housekeepers than mothers. Their letters show them taking part in the legal and business interests of the family, as well as in the purely domestic sphere where they ruled supreme.
>
> To organize the feeding and clothing of the inhabitants of one or more manor-houses was in itself a task for life, requiring the same sort of administrative ability as ladies in our day so often devote to public work or professional employment. The household requirements could not in those days be met by hasty 'shopping'. Everything that could not be supplied by the estate must be ordered in the

requisite quantities months beforehand—wines of France, sugar grown in the Mediterranean, spices, pepper, oranges, dates and the better kinds of cloth. It was the lady's business to make these provident calculations of coming needs and to see that orders were placed with solid merchants of the County capital or more often in London, for even Norwich failed to supply such overseas goods as would now be found in shops of any small market town. As to home produce, the preparation, curing and storing of the meal, meat and game off the estate and the fish from the ponds, besides the command of the dairy, the brew-house and of the kitchen with its fire of logs roaring up the great chimney, were all under the supervision of the lady chatelaine. Much of the clothing too of the inmates of the manor-house was spun and woven, cut out and made up in the house or the neighbourhood under the lady's orders. Her daughters did not go to town to buy their dresses, though one might hope to have the stuff for one's best dresses fetched from London. The young men, as brightly and fancifully clothed as their sisters, having more liberty to travel, could more often deal with a city tailor.

Thus we can imagine the innumerable and constant activities of a wealthy matron, and *mutatis mutandis* the housewife's round of work in all ranks of life.

This is the description of a work organization which is also a family enterprise, not a small family group such as is common today, but the wide network of an extended family with many servants. Each member of a family was expected to contribute what he could by working from early childhood through to old age and in return he would be looked after by other members of the family group in times when he needed help. Just as the landowners organized his family into a co-operative enterprise so did his tenants and so did the labourers. In general, most people were able to cope with social insecurity through family support unless there were big upheavals in the district such as those caused by the enclosures or by widespread epidemics.

Another protector against insecurity was the Church, and apart from their memberships of family and village this was the only organization with which most people came in close contact. Above and beyond was the state. In both church and state the ordinary people were what Etzioni calls 'the lower participants', excluded from the élite groups of clergy and politicians by lack of education and lack of capital.

In the towns the guild system of organization was perhaps a little more sophisticated, but the workshops were usually on a small scale with clearly defined authority and responsibility at the different levels of master, craftsman, journeyman and apprentice. The guilds were social organizations which provided help to their members in case of need.

This description of social organizations will be concerned very largely with work organizations, because until recently the majority of people were members of the working class whose waking lives were spent mainly in work. It was not until the nineteenth century that the middle class began to grow and to develop its own special contributions to social organizations. Meanwhile the poor worked hard and the rich led separate and very different lives. Many used their leisure in the service of the state as politicians or army officers. In the political and military organizations sponsorship was of greater importance than merit and the struggles to free politics and, later, the services from this system of interpersonal relationships has been well chronicled in the history books.

It may be useful now to consider the development of work organizations and later to examine middle-class professional associations and voluntary organizations.

The industrial revolution disturbed all the established patterns of living. Families were first drawn to work in the mills set up where there was water power and later to the coalfields or to build canals, railways and roads. There were great migrations from the country to the new towns where there were work opportunities. There, people had to learn a new way of living. The demands made by the industrial employers for long hours of work were not compatible with the old patterns of family life and many had great difficulty in adjusting to industrial discipline and the new style of living. The Hammonds called this period of adjustment 'the bleak age', because in reading records of these years they came across so much misery.

In general the people living in villages were accustomed to being treated reasonably well by their employers who saw that it was in their own interest to do so. However, this aristocratic-traditional concern had begun to break down during the eighteenth century. In England there were the enclosures, and the Speenhamland system was introduced to keep down labourers' wages. In France, the breakdown of communication between aristocrats and peasants led to political revolution and this came just at the time when the industrial revolution was adding to the disruption of the old patterns of rural social life in England.

In consequence, the new work organizations became in-volved in the political struggles about rights and responsi-bilities. The authority of the entrepreneurs was challenged by their employees. R. Bendix in his *Work and Authority in Industry,* 1963, has told how the struggle developed. The entrepreneurs who started the new businesses usually began in a small way. Often they were inventors or especially interested in the technical processes. As their businesses grew they found they needed to delegate some of their work to others. Often they brought in other members of their family to help them with problems of marketing or of managing the work force. But, when they could not get other members of the family or other reliable people among their friends to help, they might make an arrangement with a sub-contractor to carry out some of the work for them. Bendix has listed the rights and duties of the sub-contractor who

> makes employment contract with workers, makes produc-tion contract with employer, recruits and selects workers, trains and inducts workers, supervises and disciplines workers, pays workers on a time or piece basis, has a legal right to share in the profits.[1]

The aristocratic-traditional pattern of authority may be kind, it may efficient, or it may be neither. It is idiosyncratic, depending on the power figure at the top whether he be landowner, entrepreneur or sub-contractor. He may perceive it to be in his interest to be benevolently paternal to his dependents, but if he is an absentee landlord or a gambler or a money-grabbing profiteer they have no redress unless they can organize themselves to stand against him, or if they can appeal to some higher authority.

The ideology of the nineteenth century was capitalistic and *laissez-faire*, so that the idea of instituting state controls was not generally acceptable. It took many years of struggle to get protective legislation enacted to prevent the worst abuses of female and child labour and to ensure that wage payment was made in coin of the realm and not in adulterated 'truck' or alternatively liable to be squandered in public houses because it was paid there.

It was thought that adult men ought to be able to bargain for the sale of their labour to their employers and that there should be no restrictions on the making of such a contract, but the scales were weighted against employees in the early nineteenth century because they were not at the time allowed to combine against their employers. Gradually, however, during the period 1824–71 collective bargaining was established and trade unions legally constituted.

The struggle for control of work organizations in the nineteenth century was particularly concerned with the question of ownership. Robert Owen's history is one example of how muddled much of the early thinking was. He was an entrepreneur who established a model town in New Lanark, where he provided social services to his employees on benevolently paternal lines. New Lanark was particularly famous for experiments in part-time education. In addition Owen was involved in some of the early experiments in the setting up of co-operative communities where the members all shared in the ownership, the work and the production. But none of these experiments was successful. The usual reasons for breakdown of co-operative communities were personality conflicts or insufficient capital to tide over period of trade recession. He was also an active member of the Grand National Consolidated Trades Union which grew up after

57

the repeal of the Combination Acts in 1824. This union was less interested in industrial than in political action. Its main concern was to promote the Great Charter, until the Chartist campaign failed in 1848.

The trade unions took many years to sort out what kind of organizations they wanted to be. After the failure of their attempts at political action in the early nineteenth century they explored another role—that of the friendly society which collected payments from men in work as an insurance against hard times: sickness, injury, unemployment, and other disasters. Of course, friendly societies also grew up independently of the unions. Often these friendly societies met in public houses and they took names like the Odd-fellows, the Frothblowers and so on. These mutual aid organizations were very important to working people in the nineteenth century, when the harshness of the Poor Law made it important to develop all kinds of neighbourly supports in case of economic difficulties. After 1911 the state took over most of those financial activities of the friendly societies which had not already been taken over by commercial insurance companies, though some of their social concerns still remain. There are, of course, also mutual aid and philanthropic organizations, like the Masons and Rotarians, with strong middle-class orientations and international connections. However, after 1871, the unions were mainly concerned with industrial action and friendly society and political pressure-group activities became secondary to this.

The search for the solution to the social control of work organizations went on all through the nineteenth and into the mid-twentieth century. The Limited Liability Act of 1856 and subsequent Companies Acts established the system whereby only the shareholders (or in the case of firms, the partners) have legal rights in the joint stock company. However, the position of the trade unions was legalized in 1871 and, where unions became established, employers had to justify any actions connected with terms and conditions of employment to their workpeople, who formed an opposition party.

The concept of ownership by the workers themselves was

a persistent theme in the nineteenth century. Experiments were tried in producers' and consumers' co-operatives, but they proved disappointing. Others advocated syndicalism and guild socialism and there was an attempt to establish workers' self-governing syndicates in shipyards and steelworks in the First World War. However, Marxist and Russian revolutionary ideas of class warfare did not win sufficient support in Britain to bring about the complete overthrow of capitalism. The *laissez-faire* ideology had given way to the idea of control, on the one hand through union opposition, and on the other through new legislation to change the distribution of power and rewards. The Labour Party was formed in 1901 with this purpose in mind by trade unionists and other radicals. Gradually the Labour Party became identified with the policy of state ownership of the basic industries, and the Liberal Party with co-partnership. A number of companies developed profit-sharing schemes to meet the challenge from their workers.

The Labour Party nationalized a number of industries in the period 1945–51. These industries were not taken over and made part of the civil service but were put under a series of state boards, broadly responsible to a Minister of the Crown but independent in their day-to-day activities. There has been great disappointment at the failure of nationalization to solve the authority problems of these industries. G. B. Baldwin, writing about the nationalization of the coal industry in 1956, said:

> Socialists had long claimed that they would make a unique contribution to the labour problems of modern industry and this claim had been advanced with special force in the case of British coal. A decade's experience has shown this claim to be much less valid than many once believed: instead of nationalization dominating the industry's labour problems, these problems have persisted and have dominated nationalization.
>
> This judgement does not mean that nationalization has been unimportant or irrelevant. It simply means that people expected too much of nationalization and under-

stood too little about the problems of the industry. Absenteeism, recruitment, wastage, methods of wage payment, unofficial strikes, the transfer of labour, rival unionism, joint consultation—problems such as these have an existence of their own which is largely independent of the form of industrial ownership. And the way such problems are handled has more to do with a miner's performance than the old issues of private ownership and the profit motive. These issues were important to the winning of nationalization at the political and ideological level. But it has been an historical weakness of socialist thought to assume that effective economic motivations for the workshop would be supplied by the ideological symbols of a political struggle. . . .[2]

It is now generally agreed that ownership is not a major problem. Bendix's historical study went on to show that as industry grew larger and more complex the entrepreneurs had to look beyond the limits of a family concern, on the one hand to bring in more capital from shareholders and so to become public companies, and on the other to appoint managers to run their businesses. Bendix compares the situation in capitalist America and communist Russia after 'the managerial revolution' and argues that they have to face problems identical with those Baldwin has listed above.

The American sociologist Talcott Parsons has suggested that there are three levels of problem-solving in organizations:

the technical level where the product of the organization is made or the service provided is concerned with attaining the goals of the organization and adapting it to its environment, the managerial level which integrates the organization, whilst the top or institutional level (usually called the Board of Directors) related the organization to the larger society thus legitimating it and providing for pattern maintenance. The consequence is that each does not in fact 'supervise' the next lower level, for each deals with problems of a wholly different order. The major problems which organizations have to solve are: adaptation, goal attainment, integration, pattern maintenance, and tension management.[3]

Charles Perrow states his idea of a three-level system in this way:

> Organizations are influenced by three factors: the cultural system which sets legitimate goals, the technology which determines the means available for reaching these goals, and the social structure of the organization in which specific techniques are embedded in such a way as to permit goal achievement. The three factors are interdependent. When a long range view is taken, the cultural system seems determinate: when a medium range view is taken the technological system seems determinate: in the short run the structure may appear to be the most important. . . .[4]

But these ideas developed in the second half of the twentieth century. It took a considerable amount of time for social scientists to distinguish between these different strata. So far, we have been discussing the institutional level ideologies and legitimate authority; now it is important to examine the development of ideas about structure and about technology.

The first major contribution to the examination of the structure of the type of organizations which were emerging during the nineteenth century was that of the German sociologist Max Weber, writing at the turn of the twentieth century. He drew attention to the way in which bureaucratic organizations had considerable advantages over the old aristocratic-traditional (sponsorship) or charismatic models. (The charismatic organization is one led by a popular leader who carries along his followers through the power of his personality.)

Bureaucratic organizations are governed by well known rules. They are logical and rational and not irresponsible, as were Courts with favourites or many masters to their servants. One example of a well established bureaucracy is the Roman Catholic Church. In the second half of the nineteenth century most advanced national states had developed a civil service based on competitive entry. The old methods of appointment by sponsorship in the aristocratic tradition were being reviewed all over Western Europe, for there had been too many inefficient men appointed in government and military services who were later shown up in international confrontations such as the Crimean War. Weber was able to take the new civil service organizations as examples for his analysis of structures. These were the characteristics he identified:

(a) defined rights and duties which are prescribed in written regulations;
(b) authority relations between positions which are ordered systematically;
(c) appointment and promotion which are regulated and are based on contractual agreement;
(d) technical training (or experience) as a formal condition of employment;
(e) fixed monetary salaries;
(f) a strict separation of the office and the incumbent in the sense that the employee does not own the 'means of administration' and cannot appropriate the position;
(g) administrative work as a full-time occupation.

The advantages which he saw in bureaucracy were:

its technical superiority because of its greater precision, speed, lack of equivocation, knowledge of the documentary record, continuity, sense of discretion, uniformity of operation, system of subordination and reduction of functions. It provides for concentration of the means of administration, it has a levelling effect on social and economic differences, and it implements a set of authority relationships which become permanent and indispensable.[5]

Weber was convinced that this rational-legal type of organization was so logical that it would be bound to replace the less efficient forms, but not everyone is as convinced of its efficiency as he was, Red-tape, buck-passing, *bureaucratic* behaviour, clock-watching, these are all terms we use to criticize inefficient performance by bureaucratic employees, particularly if we are clients at the receiving end of some rigid civil service departments.

This seeming paradox in which the logic of efficiency resulted in efficient and inflexible action at the lower levels of some bureaucracies interested a number of political and social scientists, but it was not until the mid-twentieth century that there were real advances in understanding. Two social scientists with experience in American public services who used this experience to help their thinking were Simon and Blau. H. A. Simon's *Administrative Behaviour,* published in 1945, was concerned with the dilemmas of choice which had to be faced by large-scale organizations. Should they organize on a basis of grouping together by purposes, by processes, by clientèle or by area? And, having made this decision, how then would they link together the product groups or the area offices? How could they align their different goals? It was difficult to maximize productivity in the short term—to drive the workers hard—without jeopardizing the survival of the organization over the long term. He contrasted *maximizing* and *satisficing* and explained that this new word described the way in which most organizations behaved—they made compromises about conflicting objectives for there were dilemmas which they could not resolve.

Peter Blau, in *Bureaucracy in Modern Society,* 1956, reconsidered Weber's analysis, and he too showed the dilemmas of choice in deciding upon organization structure. To give some British examples, in a county authority there could be more small offices or fewer larger offices each with a head in charge. The decision to establish more small offices would provide more opportunities for early promotion to head but probably fewer opportunities of moving up from there, in contrast with longer hierarchical organization of the larger offices. The offices could be tightly controlled by rules imposed from head office or allowed the discretion to decide on their own methods of handling problems. Decisions could be made arbitrarily and speedily without consulting employees, or democratically and slowly after much discussion. Each of these methods has its advantages and disadvantages and would be more or less suitable in different circumstances.

Just as Simon and Blau considered the structural choices, other sociologists began to re-examine Weber's idea that all the employees at the bottom of the organization would work more effectively because bureaucracy was more rational, more just than a paternalistic organization. Alvin Gouldner studied an organization which was in the process of change from benevolent paternalism to 'more efficient' bureaucracy.[6] This organization was located in a small American town and consisted of a gypsum mine and a wall-board factory. It had been run by an elderly manager who had been flexible and paternal in his methods of supervision—if a man wanted a day off to go hunting, this was usually granted and the manager relied on loyalty to himself to see that privileges were not abused and the work was got out. However, at the head office in a distant city it was considered that the plant was not producing efficiently. It was decided that the manager should be replaced by a younger man who should take immediate steps to increase productivity. Gouldner compared the way in which the miners were able to resist major reorganization and broadly to maintain their traditional work behaviour because they could not be closely supervised with the fate of the employees in the wallboard factory who were made to obey strict rules by new foremen appointed to breathe down their necks and get more work out. The consequence was that the tension which grew up between the new manager and the men finally exploded in a wildcat strike. From his case-material Gouldner suggested that there was more than one kind of bureaucracy as perceived by the men on the shop floor. Mock bureaucracy occurred when some outside organization (such as head office) imposed rules and both management and men combined to ignore them; punishment-centred bureaucracy resulted from authoritarian decisions by management to get the work done or else ... ; representative bureaucracy was government by consent where management and workers got together to agree what were the rules to be imposed.

Subsequently, Mary Goss has suggested that there is a fourth kind of bureaucracy which can be identified and which she has called advisory bureaucracy.[7] Many people have to satisfy more than one superior although only one is the formal head of department. The others give advice which they expect to be taken into consideration in doing the job. Goss's work was mainly done in American hospitals, but an illustration of her thinking can be given from the British hospital service. The ward sister, whose immediate superior is the matron, looks to her only for help in administrative matters. These are likely to arise very infrequently if routines are well established. Much of the decision-making in her daily work depends upon the clinicians' decisions, but the doctors are her advisers only. There is a dual authority pattern. The sister is expected to take orders given by the matron as her formal departmental head, but also to comply with the clinicians' suggestions—these she has to take under critical review, but not necessarily to follow in making her decisions, but non-compliance with a physician's suggestions is a serious matter and unless she can show that she has taken all the relevant facts into consideration in deciding to ignore his advice she will not be good at her job.

But this is to suggest that all authority comes from above, from the remote rule-making agency in head office, from the departmental head, from the expert advisor, from the formal agreements made by workers and management. Other sociologists have shown that this is not so, that authority also derives from the work situation and we must now go back in time to trace the development of this other thinking about organizations. The scientific management school was another approach which stressed rationalization of effort, the application of greater logic to the organization of businesses. Urwick has described how the new professional managers, appointed in the late nineteenth century, began to examine whether they could improve the efficiency of their businesses.[8] There were men and women in America, Britain and France who wished to share their professional experience with one another so that they might take advantage of the new ideas about better organization.

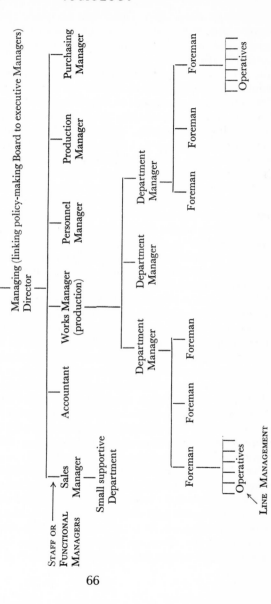

CHART I
LINE AND STAFF MANAGEMENT

Some of these ideas were about organization structure, some about the improvement of work at the technological level. Since we have been considering structures it may be useful to continue with ideas about the hierarchy.

In France in the last decade of the nineteenth century, Fayol, who was the manager of a mining organization, described how he organized the delegation of work to others by developing a hierarchy of managers. Later, in 1925, a compatriot, Graciunas, suggested that effective management depended on adequate communication within the management hierarchy and proposed that senior managers should not have more than eight managers reporting to them if they wished to have an effective span of control.

In America, during the inter-war years, two very different people made a contribution to thinking about the functions of the manager and his place in organization structure. Mary Parker Follett, a political scientist, was concerned with his role as integrator. He should be aware of 'the law of the situation' and should help his subordinates to find compromise solutions to their conflicts by helping them to see beyond their own immediate interests. Chester Barnard, a successful businessman, was also concerned about executive leadership and the difficulties in the communication processes in large organizations.

In Britain, Urwick, an ex-army officer, spread these ideas from other countries and, being convinced that the army was so much more effectively organized than were most industrial companies, suggested that they should examine their management structures and reorganize in the same way as the army, using a pyramidal structure for operational control (line management) and appointing functional specialists as staff managers or advisers, as in Chart I.

In an organization structure of this kind, the line managers are in control of the main activity of the enterprise—producing goods or services—and the staff managers have responsibility for servicing their needs by obtaining labour, materials or tools for them to use and disposing of the finished goods. The staff managers cannot give orders to the line managers, with whom they are in a mutually advisory relationship, but they are expected to maintain the steady flow of work by providing integrative services and seeing that line managers observe the rules so that their behaviour is reasonably consistent.

The proponents of scientific management thought that this form of organization was the best for all organizations, but subsequent research suggests that it is only one kind of structure, efficient for certain circumstances, but inappropriate for others. The differences are related to the technological bases of industry. Before discussing these findings, however, it is necessary to describe the other work of the scientific management school.

In Britain contributions to improved work organization were also made by managers describing their successes in planning effective store-keeping, in keeping control of costs. During the First World War the Industrial Fatigue Research Board made important discoveries about the individual's performance in work, what were the optimum conditions for lighting, heating and ventilation, what was a good length for the working day and the working week, and how breaks could increase output.

In America there were two outstanding men who applied the logic of engineering science to work processes. F. W. Taylor studied the activities of labourers at the Bethlehem Steel Co. at the turn of the century and saw that the effectiveness of their performance could be enormously improved by giving them properly designed tools and training them to eliminate wasted movements. Frank Gilbreth took this further and designed work-flow schemes in which men, tools and materials were always placed in conjunction with each other to enable production to be got out with the least effort. From the work of F. W. Taylor was developed time study and new schemes of incentive payment. In time study, old methods of piece-rate fixing by bargaining were replaced by new methods in which a time study engineer would stand over a worker and time his movements with a stop watch. After calculations were made, a time to do the job would be fixed and if the worker beat this time he would be able to earn incentive pay. The unions were very resistant to stopwatch timing at first and believed it to be another device for exploiting the workers, particularly since before 1939 there was a consistently high level of unemployment and time study seemed likely to decrease work opportunities by making the people in jobs work harder. The savings to the company were not all going to be distributed to workers but were to be shared.

In spite of this, time study was introduced and continues to be used in a considerable number of organizations, usually nowadays with workers' and unions' approval. Why then, did the unions ever come to accept time study? After the first shock of its introduction it came to be seen that, although it increased management's control over the work situation, to some extent there were still opportunities for workers to exercise some discretion. All kinds of ways of beating the system were worked out—slow motion whilst being timed, stockpiling, and so on. Often where there is an incentive scheme the supervision is lighter, and the pay usually higher. Time study has now been developed into work study and the applied science of production engineering. In a few universities the study of ergonomics, or the relationship between men and machines, is being developed. Production engineering and ergonomics would both appear to have considerable potentialities which have not yet been realized, largely because the scientists who have been developing these technologies have been unaware of the importance of the social systems which arise out of the technical systems they plan and put into operation. Carried away by the logic of their technical plans they do not recognize their implications for the social interactions among workers. In a well known article which reported on the use of mechanized coal-getting machines, E. L. Trist and K. W. Bamforth discovered that many of the miners in the pit were exhibiting all the signs of low morale or alienation.[9] The new system of coal-getting kept them isolated from one another at the coal face as they loaded the coal on to moving belts. In earlier days the miners had worked closely together in mutually supportive groups, taking it in turns to do a variety of jobs and being able to talk and laugh together. Now it was no wonder that absenteeism was high, for the comradeship was gone and apart from the pay this had been the main compensation for going underground. Later, Trist was to go on to develop the idea that there was not only one logic—the technical logic of the production engineer—but that, taking social factors into consideration, organizations had choice in their technical planning if they also considered social structures.

The advantages of scientific management were widely publicized in Britain and America. In the U.S.A. a number of Business Schools, basing their teaching on these methods, were established in universities (the first in Philadelphia in 1894) and there developed considerable support for management associations in the inter-war years. In Britain there was less enthusiasm and little action. Urwick tried, without much support, to get businessmen to set up a national management institute and to get universities and technical colleges to put on courses in management studies, and although there was an awareness during and after the Second World War that British management was not efficient, it took a long time for Urwick's ideas to be accepted. A British Institute of Management was set up in 1949 and two Business Schools in 1964. It is perhaps important to point out here that the valuation set upon social organizations depends very much on their cultural context, and although French, American and German studies have been referred to in this discussion, manufacturing organizations or the civil services have been valued very differently in the different national settings. We have had to make a complete revaluation of Britain's place in the world since 1945 and to become an industrial trading power not a colonial trading power.

The next school of thought, the human relations movement, found its greatest support in America. It seemed to offer an alternative to organized trade unionism which was later in becoming generally established in the U.S.A. and was meeting with greater resistance from strongly capitalist management than in more socialist Britain, but, more than that, it seemed to fit in with the American pattern of more active participation in local affairs and greater verbalization of feeling. At the end of the war, particularly, it fitted in with the desire of the democratic countries to find a means of managing conflict by 'working through' tensions in discussion.

The human relations school developed theories to explain why scientific management was only a partial answer to improved organization of business enterprises, but in counterbalancing the rational approach the pendulum swung too far the other way. Elton Mayo and his colleagues discovered that management's expectations were usually well understood by work groups, but it was generally more satisfying to these work group members to conform to the expectations of the group rather than to those of management. Thus the group would establish norms of behaviour—for example, what they thought was a reasonable day's output—and the members would help one another to reach that target but not to go far beyond. The only people likely to respond fully to incentive pay as a motivator would be those who did not wish to conform to the group and for personality reasons had to prove that they could achieve well as individuals.

The experiments carried out at the G.E.C. Hawthorne plant and reported by F. J. Roethlisberger and W. J. Dickson in *Management and the Worker,* 1939, demonstrated that factors such as good lighting, heating and ventilation which were known to have an effect on individual productivity could be played down by groups of workers to a very large extent if their morale was high and they were determined to produce well. This experiment and others carried out later suggested that what was important in a supervisor was that he should be employee-centred, willing to listen to his subordinates and to involve them in departmental decision-making. The tough authoritarian manager seemed to be outmoded in democratic society and especially in times of full employment. (Later experiments have questioned this thinking.)

Because of the war, there was some delay in bringing the first human relations finding to Britain across the Atlantic and the climate was not particularly receptive at the time of Mayo's visit in 1947. It was not until the end of the 1950s that there began to be general recognition of the importance of work groups. However, Mayo's visit encouraged a number of social scientists to begin to seek facilities to do their research in industry and a British school which became interested in socio-technical systems began to emerge. In America during the 1950s a number of sociologists had also begun to seek explanations for differences in the behaviour of industrial workers in different industries in terms of technological imperatives. However, Joan Woodward's British study is perhaps the most significant.[10] She discovered that the industrial organizations in south-east Essex could be arranged in a continuum according to their technical processes and that they had different organization structures which had emerged under the pressures of the technological situation unless they had been made to fit the scientific management formula: where they had been made to fit this formula there were distinct signs of strain. Line

CHART II

PRODUCTION SYSTEMS IN SOUTH-EAST ESSEX INDUSTRY

GROUP I Small-batch and unit Production	I	Production of simple units to customers' orders	(5 firms)
	II	Production of technically complex units	(10 firms)
	III	Fabrication of large equipment in stages	(2 firms)
	IV	Production of small batches	(7 firms)
	V	Production of components in large batches subsequently assembled diversely	(3 firms)
GROUP II Large- batch Production	VI	Production of large batches, assembly line type	(25 firms)
	VII	Mass production	(6 firms)
	VIII	Process production combined with the preparation of a product for sale by large-batch or mass-production methods	(9 firms)
	IX	Process production of chemicals in batches	(13 firms)
	X	Continuous flow production of liquids, gases and solid shapes	(12 firms)

(8 firms unclassified because too mixed or changing.)

Source: *Management and Technology*, D.S.I.R., 1957.

and staff organization was appropriate for mass production but not for jobbing or for process production.

J. D. Thompson has recently re-analysed the evidence about the effect of technology on organization structure.[11] He points out that the studies have mainly been carried out in manufacturing industry and whilst accepting that organization within an industry can differ, as Woodward suggests, he argues that there are other categories of work organization too. Manufacturing, he says, aims at the achievement of a long-linked technology, attaining a constant rate of production and using capacity to full extent. Commercial organizations, banks, etc., can be described as having a mediating technology: they provide the necessary communication mechanisms in modern society and try to introduce standardization and bureaucratic rules as much as possible. Hospitals, the armed services and the construction industry have an intensive or custom technology: their services have to be carried out according to demands of clients in relation to resources available. In consequence structures differ.

Thompson suggests that structures differ because, in each case, the organization tries to protect its technical core. The technical core is the reason for its separate existence, its special contribution to society. Round this core is built a domain, that is, a task-environment, which acts as a buffer against the predictable ups and downs of supply and demand whether of customers or clients; suppliers of materials, labour, capital, equipment, and work space; competitors for markets or resources; regulatory groups—government, unions, or inter-firm associations. It also takes into account the local community and the possible future environment of the organization. His division into categories is based on the concept that a different kind of structure will be required when there are more employees in boundary positions with discretionary responsibility to decide on one aspect of the organization's relationship to the community.

Like E. L. Trist, he stresses the necessity of perceiving the organization as a social system composed of a series of sub-systems and being itself a part of a larger system. The scientific management school did not see beyond the closed system

73

of the organization itself and its internal relationship problems. But, says Thompson, internal relationships are determined by external pressures. Professional employees such as doctors in hospitals are in a strong power position because the hospital is dependent upon their services, but equally they are dependent upon hospitals for the facilities they need to carry out their work—highly skilled technical assistance, specialized equipment, and so on. This positive tension does not exist in the same way in manufacturing industry.

Like Follett, Thompson sees the role of the supervisor and the hierarchy above him to help integrate the conflicting interests of subordinates. However, in larger or more complex organizations the hierarchy cannot do all the integrating that is necessary. The bureaucratic organization found that standardization through establishing rules was one way of relieving supervisors from continually having to make small decisions which were probably often inconsistent with their own previous decisions or those of the foreman in the next workshop. Standardization led to the development of functional specialist departments, such as personnel or costing departments, which were expected to advise on consistency in applying the rules throughout the organization.

However, whilst standardization could solve problems of consistency, it could not solve problems of sequence or sharing of services. Committees were set up to work out solutions to these problems and to establish the rules of a 'representative bureaucracy'. Woodward's study also demonstrated the importance of committees of experts in process industries where no one man had sufficient expertise to make decisions and had to rely on discussion with colleagues. Thompson suggests that custom technologies such as hospitals have even greater need for sharing expert views and that the concept of complexity in an organization is not coterminous with size, but with the need for mutual adjustment between the different professionals who are employed there. Thus, the line and staff organization chart is irrelevant in hospitals or local authorities which are trying to reconcile good-quality professional services with efficient use of resources, for standardized quantitative measures cannot be easily applied and good communications between the different experts are necessary so that they can see what their decisions mean in the larger context.

Thus, the open system theorists have stressed not only the need to consider the social systems and their relation to technologies within work (as the human relations school did), but also to examine the interaction between the turbulence of the environment with the way in which the task is carried out. The managers at the integrative level will seek to find ways of sealing off the task from the turbulence outside by different solutions appropriate to the needs of the organization. Thus the ice-cream plant makes sausages too in order to level off winter and summer demands; the large office block in London contracts out its cleaning to specialists because they have mechanical equipment and more knowledge of that labour market; the store has an extensive staff training programme to try to socialize its saleswomen into providing a more skilful service to customers than its rivals, or it decides not to compete on that basis at all but to allow customers great freedom of choice of a good range of merchandize displayed attractively to encourage buying but with little customer service.

Although managers are unable to control many of the factors affecting the efficient running of their businesses they continue to seek organizational rationality. Thompson suggests that there are three levels of operation. Efficiency tests are used when all the variables are known (or thought to be known) and these can be applied particularly to technological activities such as automatic production of gear wheels. Instrumental tests are set up where the variables are not all known, but a number of dimensions are constant on the more important task environment elements; their standardization (adherence to the rules) can be applied, as can scheduling or quota filling and, in the public services, rationing. Social tests are the last to be used, but it may be necessary for an organization to fall back on considering the opinion of its reference groups, the groups which are important to it, such as the clients of a social service, or the press, or the local ratepayers; evaluation is made in terms of the confidence expressed.

A number of social scientists have been concerned to explore decision-making in organizations, to discover what are the variables so that they may begin to be controlled. The scientific management group thought that by developing work study they would find the means to pin down the variables on the production line. They discovered that they had to cope with the problem of getting compliance from workers, that management's expectations and the performance they could get out were not necessarily congruent for they could not control discretion altogether. Thus there grew up recognition that there was an area of effort bargaining or silent bargaining, the indulgency pattern, a zone of indifference or a zone of acceptance, as it came to be called by the many authors who wrote about the difficulties of getting compliance. At the time when time study was introduced, labour was the flexible factor in the production situation. Labour did not become scarce until the Second World War and it was in the early 1950s that the second industrial revolution came with automation and computerization. This presents many more opportunities for developing controls over the planning of work processes, but it is only just beginning to be exploited. Calculations which were impossible before are now taken for granted, but computers are still being employed on routine work such as wages calculations or invoicing instead of diagnostic work to discover relevant variables which might be controlled in the technological situation. Enid Mumford has shown how ill prepared most of the companies are when computers are installed.[12] Large companies have established operational research departments to look for new solutions to their problems, using scientists trained in a number of different disciplines in the research team. They look for managers' rather than workers' inefficiencies.

Although ownership is no longer a real issue, participation in the running of the organization still remains the subject of sociologists' concern. A number of writers have examined the reasons for the alienation of the majority of employees in terms of the technology. These have been summarized by Blauner, who argued that technology had developed from craft industry which provided involvement, self-expression and self-esteem for the workers, through mechanized industry which was meaningless to the workers and created a sense of powerlessness, isolation and self-estrangement. He predicted that automated industry will give back the worker some control over his work and will bring him back into meaningful relation with society.[13] Dubin, on the other hand, is following up a study made ten years ago on the 'central life interests' of workers which suggests that work is no longer the major concern of most employees. (professional people are the exception). They work to live, to spend their leisure as they wish rather than finding work and work relationships the only important relationships outside the family as they were in the past.

A. Etzioni has suggested that organizations can be categorized into three types according to the patterns of compliance that they expect to get from their 'lower participants'. He has designated these: normative, remunerative or utilitarian, and compulsive organizations. The normative organization is the public service organization which has as its élite or leadership group professional people like doctors and schoolteachers. These professionals set the standards for their assistants and for their clients. They expect to get compliance because of their expertise and, because they are providing a service to the community, people will want to co-operate because it is for their own good. The remunerative organization (and most manufacturing and commercial businesses fall into this category) expects to motivate workers by financial incentives and will probably also use ideological appeals. The results of this approach are variable. Some workers respond favourably, others are noncommittal and others still are alienated. The compulsive organizations such as the army or the prison use sanctions or threat of sanctions to get compliance from their 'lower participants' whether employees or clients.

Whilst the importance of ownership has now diminished in significance the importance of participation in the running of organizations has become recognized to be increasingly worthwhile. R. Dubin puts it this way: 'The crucial factor in social power deriving from industrial technology is the ability to determine the direction in which the new technology will evolve.' But, he says, 'these decisions are not taken by managers alone but by managers in conjunction with directors of business firms, legislators, competitors, consumers and labour union officials'. The decisions he lists are 'institutional practices defining the nature of work, the division of labour among industries, investment policies and the conditions of organized stability'.[14]

The managers have had to sort out their relationships with the entrepreneurs or the directors of the public companies who employed them, and, as Parsons points out, there have developed three distinctive levels of problem-solving in work organizations: the managerial level, the technical level and the institutional level. At the institutional level the Board of Directors relates the organization to the larger society, providing for its legitimation and for pattern maintenance. Selznick and others have discussed this ideological leadership —the importance of balancing major objectives and establishing broad goals.[15] The managers at the integrative level have to translate these broad goals into day-to-day targets and to see that they are communicated in practical terms throughout the organization. Both parties have had to learn how to relate to the other and have found it easier to do so in public companies rather than in family firms where there is more role confusion (but there are still a large number of family firms).

Then there is the relationship with the unions which has already been described in part. After the unions became properly established in 1871, they were able to develop new tactics in their collective bargaining with employers. Gradually, managements came to understand what strategies and tactics they would use to increase their share of power in determining the terms and conditions of employment of their members. Procedures for collective bargaining were established which were almost as important as the substance of the bargaining, because they provided for regular reviews of wage rates and for the raising of any grievances for proper consideration.

But because British trade unionism had grown out of the old guild system it was organized on craft lines. There were usually several unions in one plant and there were difficulties in relationships between employers and union organizations and between the unions themselves. During the early part of the twentieth century some of the unions tried to get more strength through merging into larger industrial unions to form a united opposition to management, but this merging of skilled and unskilled workers was only successful in some industries and most continued on the old basis. Because there were usually several unions in one plant, negotiations for increases in basic rates were conducted at national or district levels. In consequence, national reviews of wage rates or grievances took a long time and seemed impersonal and remote. There seemed to be a need for new organization structures to improve work-people's participation in management decision-making.

Within the unions themselves there were a number of challenges to the established power structures, first in the First World War, by what came to be called the Shop Stewards' Movement, and again in the Second World War. However, by the end of the Second World War there seemed to be great apathy among the general membership of unions, and a good deal of concern among employers about the political motives of the few active union members. During the war, managements had tried to improve the structural mechanisms in their organizations in response to the union challenge and in consequence the concept of joint consultation was developed. This was to provide for members from several unions and/or non-unionists to get together in a plant to discuss their shared interests (rather than the opposing interests which were expressed in collective bargaining). Joint consultation was most popular during the Second World War when committees were formed of management and workers to discuss ways of increasing productivity, improving safety, minimizing absenteeism, in order to make a better contribution to national wellbeing. However, when the war was

SOCIOLOGY

over the shared interests again seemed less important than the conflicts.

There are many approaches to the sociology of industrial relations. Edward Gross identifies nine, most of which have already been described very briefly in this discussion of organization sociology.[16] However, the study of industrial relations has been of special interest to sociologists concerned with the inter-organizational conflicts of unions and management, but more attention is now being paid to conflicts within the unions and the management hierarchy.

A development of human relations theory, interaction theory, has been concerned with the problem of individual alienation which is related to the lack of involvement of the members of the organization. Chris Argyris has been particularly interested in explaining malfunctioning of organizations in terms of alienation or failure to involve people, but he has many critics who believe that he takes this too far. At the end of the war there was a concern with the concept of 'industrial democracy', the idea that citizens of a democratic society should be expected to be responsible in work as in leisure for contributing ideas and not only their brawn to organizations. However, despite the Jaques[17] investigation at the Glacier Metal Co., which gained international fame as a new interpretation of the underlying anxieties of workpeople, an investigation into the application of the practice of industrial democracy by committee rule, joint consultation began to fall out of favour as a solution to new structural methods for involving work-people. The company came to consider that what was required was rather a better understanding of management roles. Another general review of the practice of joint consultation seemed to indicate that it was an additional aid to better communication between management and workers rather than providing a new level of involvement in a democracy.

Subsequent work by specialists in industrial relations seems to indicate that workers may continue to challenge management control more effectively through promoting the role of their unions as an effective opposition to management. However, for an opposition to be good, the management too must

80

be strong. Many writers stress that management has been lacking in initiative in its dealings with unions, always defensive and limited in ideas.

Perhaps more important than the unions today are the professional associations. The professions emerged mainly during the nineteenth century although the Church, law and medicine were established much earlier. But in the early nineteenth century the old classical learning was challenged by the new scientific approach. H. A. Wilensky distinguishes the science-based from the belief-based professions. Both, say Carr-Saunders and Wilson in the first important study of the professions, are distinct from other occupations because their members 'have undergone specialized intellectual study and training, the purpose of which is to provide skilled service or advice to others for a definite fee or salary', they have a code of ethics to ensure 'the maintenance of a high standard of professional character and honourable practice', and the members seek to associate with each other 'because the better equipped desire that they should somehow be distinguishable'.[18] Some writers have been concerned to elaborate on the distinctive qualities of 'the professions' but H. L. Vollmer and D. M. Mills suggest that

> it seems more useful to analyse and describe occupational institutions in terms of the concept of *professionalization* assuming that many, if not all occupations may be placed somewhere on a continuum between the ideal type profession at one end and completely unorganized occupational categories or 'non-professions' at the other end.[19] Professionalization is a process which may affect any occupation to a greater or lesser degree.

The professions are important because their members in association are strong pressure groups. They may work for or against social reform. Many of the older established professions tend to be conservative, but when a profession is stirred to take social action the weight of learning and social responsibility are powerful forces towards change.

Although the state has employed professional civil servants and schoolteachers for about a hundred years, it is only since

1948, with the bringing in of extensive welfare state legislation, that there has been much discussion of the relationship of professional people as state employees to their employing organizations. T. H. Marshall, in *Citizenship and Social Class*, 1950, pointed out that the social services which were not cash-paying agencies were dependent upon the professionals for determining the quality of service to clients. In consequence, the state is very much concerned with the supply of professional manpower and has become involved in financing training programmes in those professions which seem to need to be maintained or developed. A number of enquiries have been made into scientific and technical manpower, the supply of teachers, doctors and social workers and, of course, the 'brain drain' through emigration.

The professions, like the unions and managements, are resistant to state intervention into their affairs, but the state has become particularly concerned about the stability of industry to change to meet the new situation of Britain in the present-day world now that the Empire has gone. Dubin stressed the importance of state intervention as a factor of adaptation of work organizations. In the 1960s, there has been a shift away from thinking about union/management relationships as separate and sacrosanct, not to be interfered with except in the last resort. The state has become an active influence upon business organizations not only to redetermine the limits of union/management bargaining, but to ensure more positive attention being given to the interests of citizens generally in industrial relations.

So far, most of this discussion seems to have been concerned with work organizations, but what has become particularly noticeable today is the concern not only of employees but also of clients to become involved in determining policies.

In the nineteenth century the middle classes had made a contribution not only to the development of entrepreneurial and professional activities, but also as philanthropists to the organization of social services for the poor. Earlier it had been sufficient to make provision by bequests or in wills for charity to be doled out by the clergy or hospitals or lawyers, as appropriate. By the mid-nineteenth century many middle-class women had taken over the work of ministering to the poor and the sick, some becoming professional nurses, teachers or, later, social workers. Others did this work on a voluntary basis and it became highly organized under the leadership of such people as Florence Nightingale or Octavia Hill, to take two examples in this field.

Thus voluntary organizations in Britain were of two kinds, the philanthropic which might be staffed by volunteers or by professionals but had a voluntary policy-making and fund-raising committee, and the mutual-aid organizations such as the friendly societies, unions and professional associations which have already been described. In 1948 many British philanthropic associations became outmoded by the welfare state provisions. Those which have survived have tended to become highly commercial in their public relations in order to raise funds. Beveridge reviewed the position of the voluntary organizations then to see what contribution they might make and suggested that what was needed was more concern for the lonely and more help to be given to the ill-educated or unimaginative in the use of leisure.[20] And, after twenty years out of fashion, voluntary organizations are being encouraged to do the many things that professional social workers cannot take time to do, mainly in terms of friendly help.

As yet, it is perhaps less obvious in Britain than in America that we are at the beginning of a tremendous surge of interest in client involvement both in state and voluntary organizations. There, the poor people march on Washington to demonstrate their feelings of frustration about the lack of communication between the bureaucratic welfare agencies and themselves and their real needs, but student unrest is an international phenomenon.

The 1960s have seen a great change in authority patterns everywhere, so that people who were once prepared to be disciplined into submission now protest vigorously about their treatment and often with good reason. Thompson has suggested that studies of complex social service organizations show that complexity is not so much a matter of size as of the number of boundary occupations, and by this he means

83

outward-facing occupations involving client relationships of various kinds which are particularly evident in the growing number of social service organizations.[21] Studies of student unrest would seem to show that the relationship of responsible senior teachers and students has broken down because of larger classes, the use of inexperienced tutorial assistants and graders of work who come between them. There is also greater interest in research and publication than in teaching students in universities. Sociologists think that the boundary positions in the organization (i.e. where it relates to clients) are becoming less well integrated.

In the past, the organization with important boundary jobs to fill has either appointed skilled professionals or has developed strong training programmes to socialize the employees who will be representing the organization. One question which has interested sociologists is the problem of loyalties of professionals, who often prefer to identify with other professionals in their occupational association rather than with other employees of the organization and thus may not be very involved with an organizational identity.

In the last few years the problem of maximizing the contribution of the professionals, both technical and managerial, in government employment, whether in the civil service or in local government, has been the subject of a number of reports. The difficulties of improving interprofessional relationships are also being faced in many organizations. It would appear that making the best use of professionals as employees is a major problem to be solved in the next ten years.

It has not been possible to consider political parties, military organizations, hospitals, schools and prisons within the scope of this chapter, but all these are variant forms of organization which have been studied and described by sociologists as well, and, although most of the work has been done on industrial organizations in the past, it seems likely that there will be more concern with these others in the future.

SOCIAL ORGANIZATIONS

SUGGESTED READING

GOULDNER, A. W., *Patterns of Industrial Bureaucracy* (Routledge & Kegan Paul, 1955).
BARNARD, CHESTER, *The Functions of the Executive* (Cambridge, Mass.: Harvard University Press, 1951).
ETZIONI, AMITAI, *A Comparative Analysis of Complex Organizations* (Glencoe, Illinois: Free Press, 1961).
ALLAN, FLANDERS, *Industrial Relations: What's Wrong with the System?* (Institute of Personnel Management, 1966).
BLAU, P. M., and SCOTT, R. W., *Formal Organizations* (Routledge & Kegan Paul, 1963).

NOTES

1 R. Bendix, *Work and Authority in Industry* (New York: Wiley, 1956).
2 *Beyond Nationalization* (Harvard University Press & Oxford University Press, 1955).
3 *The Social System* (Tavistock Publications, 1951).
4 'Hospitals: Technology, Structure and Goals' in *A Handbook of Organizations*, edited by J. G. March (Chicago: Rand McNally, 1965).
5 H. H. Gerth and C. W. Mills, *From Max Weber: Essays in Sociology*, *op. cit.*
6 *Wildcat Strikes* (Routledge & Kegan Paul, 1955).
7 'Patterns of Bureaucracy among Hospital Staff Physicians' in *The Hospital in Modern Society*, edited by E. Freidson (Collier-Macmillan, 1963).
8 L. F. Urwick and E. F. L. Brech, *The Making of Scientific Management* (Pitman, 1949).
9 *Human Relationships*, Vol. IV, No. 1, 1951.
10 *Industrial Organization: Theory and Practice* (Oxford University Press, 1965).
11 *Organizations in Action* (New York: McGraw Hill, 1967).
12 *Living with a Computer* (Institute of Personnel Management, 1966).
13 *Alienation and Freedom* (Chicago University Press, 1964).
14 *The World of Work* (New Jersey: Prentice-Hall, 1958).
15 *Leadership in Administration* (New York: Harper & Row, 1957).
16 'Industrial Relations' in *A Handbook of Modern Sociology*, edited by R. E. Faris (Chicago: Rand McNally, 1964).
17 E. Jacques, *The Changing Culture of a Factory* (Routledge & Kegan Paul, 1951).
18 Sir A. Carr-Saunders and P. A. Wilson, *The Professions* (Oxford University Press, 1933).
19 *Professionalization* (New Jersey: Prentice-Hall, 1966).
20 Lord Beveridge, *Voluntary Action* (Allen & Unwin, 1948).
21 *Op. cit.*

4

Small Communities

James Littlejohn

Sociologists have offered many definitions of *community,*
none of which have been unanimously accepted. The concept
was introduced into sociological discourse in the last century
mainly as an aid to conceptualizing, by contrast, some of the
general features of nineteenth-century industrial society.
Many sociologists then felt that this society was something
new, unprecedented and by no means wholly adequate to
what they took to be certain deep-rooted needs and tendencies of human nature, particularly the need to experience a
solidarity with one's fellows transcending any selfish interest
one might have in associating with them. To bring into
relief the distinctive features of industrial society they developed a contrast between community and association,
Gemeinschaft and *Gesellschaft* in Ferdinand Tönnies book
of that title, first published in 1887. In their writings community as a form of social life is described as a kind of
spontaneous and natural mode of integration as against the
kind of integration achieved on the one hand by the state
and on the other by the market. The state achieves integration through conscious regulation, co-ordination and, if need
be, coercion, guided by clearly formulated laws and statutes.
In contrast community integration is based on bonds of
kinship, on the sharing of a common language, religion or
culture, or simply on the bonds that form among people who
live in close proximity to each other. A diffuse solidarity
precedes any particular relationship flowing from it.

In a market economy, each man is expected to pursue his

own individual interest, understood as maximization of material gain, by buying in the cheapest market and selling in the dearest. Market operations are conducted through contracts, whereby each party specifies in greater or lesser detail the terms on which he will enter into an exchange. The operations of all the individuals in the market can be summed up as the forces of supply and demand, the relative intensities of which fix the values of commodities, including human labour. On the other hand, where community integration obtains the market is either irrelevant (as in the exchanges of words between common language speakers), or the impersonal forces of supply and demand are limited in scope. Limitation may result from sharing property and resources; from infrequency of exchange, as, say, among subsistence farmers; from that interest in each other's welfare sometimes formed among people sharing many common interests, or from some combination of these factors. Such ideas on the nature of community received apparent empirical backing from researches by economic historians into pre-feudal Teutonic and Scandinavian society, based, they held, on the township, an autonomous group of families exercising a common proprietorship over a definite tract of land. The idea of *a* community, of a bounded local group with specific characteristics, as opposed to the concept of community as a mode of integration, became widely current in Britain through the publication of Sir Henry Maine's *Village Communities in the East and West,* 1871. In these lectures he tried to show that the community represented a stage in the history of the Indo-European peoples; he held that the contemporary Indian village had all the principal characteristics of the old Teutonic township, 'the same double aspect of a group of families united by the assumption of common kinship, and of a company of persons exercising joint ownership of land' (p. 12). We shall see below that this view of the Indian village is not correct.

Note that both these strands of thought, theoretical and empirical, are linked in the current sociological conception of the community, which we may take to mean a local group, within which can be observed social bonds and activities exempt from strict regulation by contracts and co-ordination by the state, or which in a sense precede contract and supervision by the state, as in the case of normal family and kinship relations. In conformity with the explication of the concept given above I shall consider the community first in societies which lack both a state organization and a market economy; second in societies which have a state organization but not a market economy, or in which the market is limited in scope; and third in societies such as our own which have both a state organization and a market economy. For convenience I shall call these primitive, peasant and industrial societies respectively.

The Primitive Society

Here the division of labour is minimal, with only a distinction between men's work and women's work, and, lacking state organization, there is no body of men separate from the others authorized to maintain law and order or to legislate on behalf of the others. The population is distributed among a congeries of local communities, hunting bands or horticultural settlements, united partly through sharing a common language and culture but mainly through a circulation of women as brides among them in consequence of the rules composing their systems of kinship and marriage. The circulation of women entails a circulation of goods and services, not regulated by a market, but by the rules of gift exchange.

Consider the Siane of New Guinea, described by Salisbury in *From Stone to Steel*. Each village is composed of a clan, i.e. a number of people considering themselves to be descended from a common ancestor. The clan is further subdivided into lineages, smaller groups tracing descent from a known common ancestor, and lineages into households. Each clan-village is exogamous, i.e., those born into it may not marry each other, so that daughters of the clansmen at marriage go to live elsewhere with their husbands, while wives are brought in from other clan-villages. Surrounding each village is a tract of land which is its inalienable property; no part of it may be given away to another village.

Each lineage has the right to use a portion of the village land and each household a portion of its lineage land. Kinsmen help each other with the heavier tasks of cultivation, i.e. they exchange labour service without reckoning up exactly how much each gives or receives. Similarly there is continual exchange of food among them. An individual who did not join in these exchanges would be ostracized, i.e. he would lose the benefits of extra labour at the times when he needed it. The principle of gift exchange is reciprocity.

Individuals own trees, i.e. have sole rights to dispose of the fruits and nuts, though not the right to give their trees to anyone outside the clan. In harvesting nuts each calls upon the help of his mother's brother, the person who gave his father a wife. The mother's brother, by the rule of exogamy, must be a member of another village. For his help the maternal uncle gets a share of the harvest, or perhaps some other gift. One may help him with his harvest in turn, and be similarly recompensed, and of course in due time one becomes a mother's brother oneself. Individuals are also entitled to the skins of animals and birds they have killed, to salt, and to tobacco they have themselves grown. Each man creates a network of trade partners for himself in neighbouring villages with whom he exchanges these products. The aim of these exchanges is not profit in the sense of a maximization of gain—one is not free to sell one's trade-items in an open market, one must exchange only with one's trade partners, many of whom in any case are affinal relations, like one's maternal uncle. The aim is simply to ensure that one can get a particular scarce item at the particular time one wants it.

Yet there is intense competition among men, or at least among ambitious men, for prestige. It is conducted as follows. Clans have to give each other women as wives. Wives are the most valuable gifts, and in reciprocation clans have to give each other feasts, presentations of pigs and other valuables handed over with great ceremony at a joint meeting. Now the amount that each man contributes to a clan feast is carefully noted, for the more the individual contributes the more he increases his prestige. By acquiring prestige

89

SOCIOLOGY

a man gains influence in community affairs. He does not become a chief with statutory powers, but he becomes a leader, an opinion-former who may be asked to settle disputes within his community. The process is a common one in primitive societies, where one becomes a leader by giving away wealth.

With only slight exaggeration we can say that in these societies each community is like every other community, and each contains within it all the institutions of the whole society. One of the advantages anthropologists derive from this state of affairs is that by close study of one community, including its relations with others, they are able to show how the institutions of the society are functionally inter-related, how they inter-connect to form a social system. Let us take as an example the people of Dobu, an island of the Dentrecasteaux group off the north-east coast of New Guinea. Among them the rule obtains that one must not marry a cross-cousin. Cross-cousins are children of siblings of opposite sex; we can represent the situation thus:

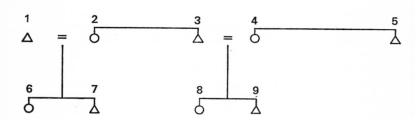

A triangle stands for a male, a circle for a female. Horizontal lines represent siblingship and vertical lines descent. The *equals* sign represents 'married to'. So 6 and 7 are cross-cousins to 8 and 9; among Dobuans they may not marry. Why not? A preliminary understanding, though not a complete explanation, can be won by noting how this rule is linked with others, and with ideas and activities in a unified social system. We can start with rules of descent, inheritance and succession. Dobuans trace descent matrilineally, and a person inherits land not from his father but from his mother's brother. Thus 7 inherits not from 1, but from 3. Now if cross-cousin marriage were permitted, e.g. if 7 married 8, this would mean that 3 would have one of his children married to his heir. This would create difficulties for the married pair as soon as 3 died, for another rule of Dobuan society is that the children of a dead man may not eat food grown on the dead father's land. Land is owned in the first instance by the village and divided out among its constituent units. The relevant point here is that a man's child is not a member of his village—one inherits rights of citizenship (so to speak) from one's mother's brother; one succeeds to his status, hence belongs to his village, which of course is also that of his sister, one's own mother. Thus the constituent units of the village are not families, but matrilineal lineages which Dobuans call *susu*. Thus 2, 3, 6 and 7 constitute a *susu,* as against a family, 1, 2, 6 and 7, for example. (The number of persons in actual lineages or families may of course be much larger than those represented in the diagram.)

Though the *susu* is the group within which rights to land and residence are transmitted from one generation to another, the family is the group which lives and works together. All the *susu* in a village are related to each other by descent from a common ancestress, and the village itself forms an exogamous group. It follows that spouses come from different villages. In which village should the family live? They solve this problem by living alternately one year in the wife's village and one year in the husband's. Now this custom would be impossible to realize if cross-cousin marriage were permitted, for another rule of residence-succession is that a child may not enter the village of his dead father; so if 7 and 8 were to marry, 8 would be unable to live with her husband every alternate year after 3 had died. This would create further difficulties since the family is both a producing and consuming unit. One can follow out in all spheres of Dobuan culture linkages between the ban on cross-cousin marriage and other institutions. For example, magic for growing yams specific to each *susu* is also transmitted from maternal uncle to sister's son, and as they believe that yams do not grow without the use of their specific magic, there would be no point in trying to take over one's father's land by force—one would not have the requisite magic of production. In any case the attempt would involve one in a feud with one's father's true heir, i.e., his sister's son, helped by the members of his *susu*. In this society there are no governmental officials, no legislators, judges or policemen. Each *susu* and village has to be prepared to defend its rights against others, by force if need be.

This is merely a sketch of the Dobuan social system, but enough perhaps to show that the ban on cross-cousin marriage is inextricably linked with other features of the system, such that if the ban were to be rescinded the system would have to alter in other ways as well; it would no longer be the same system. Finally, it is worth noting that sentiments are to a large extent given direction and object by social organization. Affections and loyalties are stronger among members of the *susu* than among members of the family. Fathers are not notably affectionate towards their wives' children, while husband and wife are constantly quarrelling, accusing each other of witchcraft and sorcery. Divorce rates are high.

In a society such as this roles are relatively undifferentiated; each adult man makes a living in the same way as the others, and there is no division among them into, for example, employers and employees. Each is an economic entrepreneur, a father, teacher, priest or magician, advocate, and so on. The structure of the society is accordingly composed of a few statuses or positions and relations among them; position by sex, descent (and generation) and marriage. Hence the social anthropologist, in his study of the community in such a society, devotes most of his attention to the system of kinship and marriage by which people are classified and related to each other.

The Peasant Society

Peasant societies differ from each other as widely as do primitive societies. Generally speaking, their technology or productive organization is more efficient than that of primitive societies; their tools are of metal, or there is some elementary economic specialization. What marks them off from primitive societies, however, is this, that a peasant society always contains non-peasants, people who do not, like the majority, hoe or till the soil for a living. These non-peasants are either government officials or townsmen or both. Simplifying radically, we may place peasant societies along a polarity at one end of which the fate of the peasants is determined by their subjection to a state organization, at the other by their economic subjection in a market economy.

At the political end of the polarity a market economy is either absent or relatively small in scope. The various local communities among which people are distributed are subject to rule by a state organization, an organization of officials who have the duty of implementing the policies and programmes of a central authority, a king, emperor, senate or council of some kind. The state maintains law and order within its boundaries and protects the community against invasion. Its main interest as regards the peasantry is in the extraction from it of surplus production, sufficient to maintain its head of state, officials and their establishments. Extraction may take the form of labour *corvées,* tithes, taxes or a combination of these. Hence the modes of both political and economic integration differ from those found in primitive societies. In the latter economic integration is achieved principally through gift exchange; there is in one sense no political integration, only cultural uniformity among a congeries of communities each responsible for defending its rights against the others. In another sense, however, since each is entitled to use force in defence of its rights, we can say that political integration is diffuse, it is achieved through organizations not specifically devoted to that end, through community and kinship organization. In the former, economic integration takes the form of redistribution, while

93

political integration is the specific task of the state, which abrogates to itself sole rights to the use of force, the ultimate sanction in the maintenance of integration.

One of the outstanding features of this kind of society is a principle of organization not found in the primitive societies, viz. stratification, the separation of persons not by membership of different but like and equal kinship groups and settlements, but by membership of classes among which wealth, power and opportunity are unequally distributed. At the same time the peasants in each village or settlement remain organized among themselves largely in terms of kinship, and have their own solidarity based on kinship and local ties. 'Community' and 'Society' now refer to distinct entities integrated in terms of distinct principles.

S. F. Nadel describes such a situation in his book, *A Black Byzantium,* 1942, an account of the Nupe kingdom of Central Nigeria, comprising several tribal populations with differing cultures but united by allegiance to the Nupe king. State officials are appointed by him from among the members of his own and two other royal lineages, and of his household, many of whom were formerly slaves. Mallams educated in Islamic law form a distinct class from which judges are appointed. In the capital merchants and guilds of craftsmen flourish, supplying the wants of the court, the nobility and the town population in general. Officials are rewarded by the allocation to them of prebendal fiefs, i.e., villages or districts from which they are entitled to collect taxes. Members of the royal lineages in addition own private domains. Officials and nobles are expected to exercise a supervisory role over their domains and fiefs, though often they leave the bulk of administration to their stewards. The state is ultimately responsible for law and order and punishes for murder and other serious crimes, for failure to pay taxes, for treason and crimes of lese-majesty, disrespect towards the king.

A typical village comprises perhaps a thousand people. The basic social unit is the extended family, a group of (mostly) patrilineal relatives under a head. Normally the head has several wives and in addition to them and their children the group includes his younger brothers with their

94

wives and children, his married sons' wives, unmarried sisters and elderly relatives unable to maintain a separate house. Each extended family occupies its own walled compound within which separate dwellings are alloted to various units, nuclear families or senior wives and children.

The ruling of village affairs is in the hands of a council composed of these family heads, one of whom, with the title of *town-king,* is chairman of the council, a position which in some villages is hereditary in one family. The duties of the council are to maintain good behaviour in the village, organize village ceremonies, particularly annual fertility rites, and to ensure that sufficient land is allocated to each compound. Round each village stretches land that only its members may cultivate. The village head in council apportions areas to compound heads who in turn apportion farms to adult men in their families.

The family head, who represents family members in village politics, is responsible to the council for the good behaviour of family members. He is also responsible for ensuring that his family members are fed, clothed and married. These duties he discharges partly by allocating land to the adult males but also by organizing the cultivation of a family farm, to which the adult males and boys must contribute labour. The produce from the family farm forms a general store from which the others can draw if need be. Most important, it is the produce of the family farm that enables the young men of the family to marry. One gets a wife from another family and, by way of recompense for the loss the other family sustains, one hands over bridewealth, cloth and valuables of various sorts (including nowadays usually a sum of money). Most marriages are contracted within the village or a small cluster of neighbouring villages, so that dense networks of kinship ties connect villagers. Behaviour is controlled largely by these ties. Towards in-laws one has to behave with respect and circumspection, else they might take back one's wife; in any case they become grandparents, uncles and aunts to one's own children. Towards the head of one's family one similarly behaves in a respectful way, as he allots one land and raises one's bridewealth, while one

95

co-operates continually in farm work with the other members of one's family. Social life in the community is controlled not by laws sanctioned by force, but by reciprocal rights and obligations linking individuals in customary ways in networks of personal relationships. Village unity is ensured not only through the institution of the council and collective ceremonies expressing a common interest in fertility, but also through the institution of age-grades.

These unite the youth of the village across their separate ties to their own families. There are three grades, the society of the little ones (10–15 years), of the boys (15–20 years), and of the young men (20–30 years). Each society of age-mates lasts about five years, is then dissolved and reformed as a society of the next highest grade. The inauguration of a society is a festive occasion, when fathers have to supply food and beer for a feast. These age-grades supply co-operative labour to whoever requires it, in hoeing or house-building, for example. The farmer has to supply food, beer and music to the company every day he hires them. The members of a grade have customary duties towards each other for life; they have to give gifts and attend ceremonies at the important crises in each other's lives—marriage, childbirth and death. In general they are expected to maintain the prestige and solidarity of their fellowship.

The peasants are subject to the state through the fiscal policies of the latter and its ultimate responsibility for law and order. However, peasant families or individuals, largely in order to protect themselves to some extent against the state, form ties of a personal nature with individual members of the upper classes, or from among the ranks of lesser officials and stewards. These in turn seek patrons in the ranks above themselves so that patron-client relations link individuals in the different strata in reciprocal services, from which no doubt the higher rank benefits more than the lower. The patron is expected to protect his client in official dealings with the state and from acts of aggression by other members of the official and noble classes. In return the client maintains the relationship by regular gifts and by in general supporting the interests of his patron in the latter's political intrigues. A peasant client who leaves his home village to be closer to his patron in the capital might, if he proves useful enough, win promotion to the ranks of officialdom.

The family, the community, stratification and patron-client relations are recurring themes in the literature on peasant societies and peasants, though the relationships these terms denote are combined in different ways in different cultures. The peasantry of southern Europe are described in these terms, for example, for Spain by J. Pitt-Rivers in *People of the Sierra*, 1954, for Greece by J. K. Campbell in *Honour, Family and Patronage*, 1964. There, as in Nupe-land, patron-client relations and stratification link peasant communities to the nation. An unusual configuration of relationships is found in India, where stratification and patron-client relations are internal to the community, features of community organization itself. The community here is not necessarily one village, but often a few contiguous ones. The community is divided in ranked groups called *jati*, usually translated as caste. A caste consists of a number of unilineal descent groups (and families) associated with and named after (often) a particular occupation, and exercising moral, religious, and social control over its members through a caste council. The occupational names are those one could expect in a basically agrarian society with a fairly advanced division of labour: Potter, Barber, Smith, Weaver, Washerman, and so on. Not all the members of a caste necessarily engage in their traditional occupation, but the point is that no one else may do so; one inherits the right to a particular occupation. At the same time agriculture is open to all castes, so that, depending on the nature of the local economy, one may find members of all castes engaged in agriculture, whether as owners of land, tenant farmers or labourers. However, castes are by no means equally represented in these three economic functions.

Castes are ranked by reference to their relative purity and impurity, concepts elaborated in a systematic theology too complex to be summarized here. We may say that impurity results from continual contact with defiling substances, particularly excretions from the human body, corpses both

SOCIOLOGY

animal and human, and some live animals such as pigs.
Many caste occupations involve such continual contact, for
example that of the Swineherd, the Washerman, the Tanner,
and others involved in disposing of carcasses. The highest
castes are priests (Brahmans) and the lowest those such as the
Tanners, often called in English Untouchables because
bodily contact between them and members of the higher
castes pollutes the latter, who then have to undergo puri-
factory ritual to remove the pollution.

Separation of the castes as distinct groups is observable
in many spheres of life. It is for example reflected in settlement patterns: caste members usually live in neighbouring
houses, and often streets are named after the castes occupying them. Untouchables always inhabit a separate hamlet
some distance from the others, and are forbidden to use the
wells and other public utilities of the others. It is also
observable in respect of commensality and connubium. That
is to say one cannot accept food from a lower caste without
being polluted, nor marry into one, at least as regards one's
principal wife, the one who produces one's legal and full
heirs. On the other hand a lower caste may try to marry
its daughters to men of a higher caste in order to raise its
status. Marriage here is accompanied not by bridewealth
(a gift from groom's family to bride's) but by dowry, a gift
of jewellery, land or money from the bride's family to the
groom's. By offering extra large dowries a caste may succeed
in this move. However, marriages and all other inter-caste
relationships are supervised by caste-councils, and the
majority of marriages are between descent groups within the
caste.

Each community is dominated by one particular caste,
which owns most of the land, sometimes all of it, and is
usually numerically the largest single caste. The dominant
caste also controls the community politically. It is usually
not a Brahman caste, though in some South Indian communities the Brahmans, the most prestigious caste in the
purity-impurity scale, are also the dominant landowners and
local political overlords. Local integration is secured not only
by the authority of the dominant caste, but also by complex

networks of hereditary patron-client relations linking families of the dominant caste with families of the others. Thus the Carpenter families will each have several patrons among the landowning caste families for whom they make and repair farm equipment; the Potter likewise. The Untouchables are farm labourers on the landowners' farms. The services which the lower castes give are not only economically productive ones but also religious. They have essential duties to perform at the ritual in which their masters are continually involved, but particularly at birth, marriage and death. The Barbers and the Washermen are particularly important on these occasions, as only the former can purify men's bodies and the latter their vestments. Brahmans too have to serve the families of the dominant caste.

In return the dominant caste rewards the others with concessions of various kinds and foodstuffs. Concessions may take the form of rights to cultivate a few acres, to houses, rights to fish ponds and tanks, to graze animals and so on. The foodstuffs consist mainly of the staple crop of the district, though now, when some peasants grow cash crops, money may be substituted for food payments. Whatever form it takes, payment is fixed at a customary rate and does not vary according to 'the state of the market', which indeed is precluded by these arrangements.

Maine's view of the Indian village is far from the truth. The families composing it, far from assuming a common kinship, are separated by caste endogamy, and they do not exercise joint ownership of land. Maine probably arrived at his characterization through considering the village only in relation to fiscal policies of the regional kings, or *rajas*. These kings in levying taxes treated the village as a unit for the purpose of tax collection, i.e., they simply demanded a fixed sum from the dominant caste, and left it to the latter to apportion contributions from its constituent families.

It is apposite to remark here that many students of peasant society have overstressed the harmonious integration of the community, largely through ignoring conflict and clash of sectional interests within it. The Indian village for example is by no means a model of harmonious integration; lower castes often contest the rulings of the dominant caste, and the latter is often ruthless in protecting its interests, beating and sometimes killing Untouchables who transgress the rules maintaining separation of castes and the position of the higher ones. At the same time the dominant caste, though presenting a united front against threats to its position, is often divided into factions. Sometimes these political factions resort to violence as a means of settling differences, on which occasions their clients among lower castes are expected to take sides with their respective masters.

However, the view of the Indian community as a self-sustaining complete micro-society has something to recommend it. Within the village are deployed all the modes of political action : discussion of policies affecting the community, adjustment of relationships, intrigue and violence. This, together with intra-community exchanges of goods and services and rigorous subjection of the individual to caste control, promotes a purely local integration which, however far from an ideal state of harmony it may be, accounts to a large extent for the remarkable durability of the caste system.

Complete lack of integration on the other hand seems to be characteristic of some Italian peasant communities, as described, for example, by Edward C. Banfield in *The Moral Basis of a Backward Society*. Montegrano is a commune of 3,400 people, mostly peasant farmers and labourers. Though it has an elected council, there is no local agency possessing political authority. The council cannot initiate policies or projects, it can only put up proposals to the nearest representatives of the state bureaucracy, who make the final decisions affecting the community. There are no community activities, no associations aiming to improve services or even to mobilize public opinion concerning them. Banfield argues that this situation results from a syndrome he calls 'amoral familism'. Each family claims the total and exclusive loyalty of its members, so that no one will further the interest of the community except as it is to his private advantage to do so. Moreover, as other families are relatively the worse off for any one family's gain, each is at best indifferent, at worst hostile, to other's attempts to maximize gain. Only officials concern themselves with public affairs, being paid to do so, but as they are appointed from outside have little interest in the community.

Both primitive and peasant communities are profoundly affected when a market economy inducts their personnel into its cash nexus. It is impossible to generalize about these effects since they differ according to the precise organization of the communities concerned, their economies, and the particular manner in which the market economy makes its impact on the indigenous organization. In Melanesia, for example, plantations drew from the villages the young men capable of sustained labour. The wages they earned enabled them to become to some extent independent of their elders, for example in raising a bride-price, so that traditional patterns of authority and leadership were weakened. In many parts of Africa the introduction of cash crops and improved techniques of cultivation (the latter obviate reliance on kinsmen or age-grades for labour) has narrowed the range of necessary co-operation among kinsmen and villagers, so weakening kinship and village solidarity. In pre-communist China the following situation developed, described by H–T. Fei in *Peasant Life in China,* 1947. Most peasants possess little capital beyond land and implements. A bad harvest means that the poorer ones have to borrow to avoid starvation or to get production going the following year. The Chinese peasant borrowed money from town merchants at high rates of interest paid in grain. The peasant remained secure in his rights to cultivate his land, but the title to it was handed over as security to the creditor. As town merchants had few outlets for investing spare capital apart from land, a market in titles developed in the towns. This pushed up the price of titles with a consequent ever-increasing rise in interest rates. Near large towns the majority of peasants were in effect labouring to enrich merchants while barely able to sustain themselves and their families. This situation along with a general breakdown of law and order in many areas explains the peasants' support for the revolutionary movement.

The Modern Society

In peasant societies community and state represent different modes of social integration. The state normally includes as subjects people of diverse or varying cultures, a nation; yet, though communities may vary in culture or economy from each other, the community is recognizably different in organization from the state and the majority of people inhabit well-defined local communities. The local community can no longer be used as a representative social field by the investigator, but at the same time he must use the community as a social framework within which to observe those relationships and institutions which control so much of the behaviour of the majority of the population.

In modern industrial society we find a different and more complex situation. Here the dominant social processes are industrialization, urbanization and bureaucratization. As a result of these and of extensive population movement, large numbers of people live in conurbations or large towns whose inhabitants are for the most part strangers to each other. True, they share common services, e.g. transport, water, etc., but the supply of these and the co-ordination of activities is achieved through impersonal administrative unities. The supply of daily needs is mediated by a host of petty contracts (as when one buys bread in a shop), connecting through money-exchange numerous persons in diverse occupations whom the individual never meets. People migrate from their place of birth in search of better jobs, so that kinship ties lapse. The vast majority of people do not own land or productive property to pass on to heirs, and jobs are acquired not through kinship connections but by learning the requisite skills. One no longer co-operates with kinsmen and neighbours in the necessary tasks of making a livelihood, nor does one of necessity spend one's leisure time in the company of workmates. In this situation and with the increasing extension of welfare services supplied by the state, government agencies assume responsibilities (e.g. the care of the aged) formerly discharged by kinsfolk. In short we have a situation in which the local community becomes ever more irrelevant

102

as a unit in society, while at the same time the state performs some of the functions formerly discharged within it. At the same time a sizable minority of the population inhabit small towns, villages and rural parishes, while modes of social life resembling in some ways those of the local community have been described for particular quarters of various towns or conurbations.

The consequences for sociological study of the community are: first, that study of the community will not enable the student to trace out the inter-relationships of the major institutions of our society : second, that there is a great variety of kinds of community, e.g. farming, mining, the village in the town, the commuter village, etc., and none can be taken as representative of the others. Or rather, it is always questionable just what any one community is representative of. For these reasons many sociologists argue that community studies are of no value for an understanding of our society. However, not all sociologists take this view. In some areas of life social relations are still exempt from or precede strict regulation by contract or the state, for example kinship relations, relations between the sexes, status-group relations, and those relations which unite people in neighbourhood leisure-time activities. These relationships, to be sure, do not or only rarely—apart from some rural communities mentioned below—produce the high degree of local solidarity which is the hallmark of the community in most primitive or peasant societies. At the same time study of them within a local setting has added considerably to our understanding of them; it has also introduced a new concept into sociological analysis, that of the social network. The idea of the network was conceived by J. A. Barnes as an aid to analysis of interpersonal relationships in modern communities where many such relationships are not formed within the context of a bounded group such as the lineage or age-grade. In modern community studies, however, we must distinguish, as C. M. Arensberg and S. T. Kimball pointed out in *Culture and Community,* 1965, between the community as the object of study and the community as the milieu within which certain relationships or activities are examined, such as

103

kinship relations or leisure activities. We shall begin with the latter perspective.

The value of milieu studies was demonstrated by the publication in 1957 of *Family and Kinship in East London* by M. Young and P. Willmott. Until then the commonly held view among sociologists was that kinship in modern society was synonymous with the nuclear family of husband, wife and children; other kinship ties were held to be of little or no importance, while the functions of the family were thought to be merely those of procreating and socializing children. The authors found that in working-class Bethnal Green the picture is more complicated and kinship ties richer in content than had been supposed. Recognition of kinship spreads far beyond the family, and where kinsfolk reside near each other effective ties do also, controlling the individual's patterns of leisure activity and comprising a network which confers social identity on him and provides a source of service he (or more often she) can call upon when required. The focal position in kinship, however, is that of the *Mum,* and the key relationship is that between mother–married daughter–grandchildren. It is through their relationship to *Mum* that siblings and their children continue to maintain relations among themselves. This bond is not merely founded on sentiment but on the help and advice *Mum* gives her married daughter, particularly at such crises as childbirth, but also whenever domestic services are required, e.g. if the daughter takes a job. Often indeed the mother finds a house for the couple when her daughter marries, and more generally acts as agent for her children in dealings with public authorities. The general pattern has been found elsewhere; J. Mogey found in his study of St Ebbs, a district of Oxford, (*Family and Neighbourhood,* 1956) that the typical St Ebbs girl brings her husband to live near her mother in her own natal district. Several other studies confirm the general picture presented for Bethnal Green, for example R. Firth's report in *Two Studies of Kinship in London,* 1956.

An outstanding study is that of W. M. Williams, reported in *A West Country Village, Ashworthy,* 1963. There the family farm is the primary social and economic unit. The farm family relies heavily on its own manpower, but naturally the adequacy of this source varies according to the size of the farm and the stage the family is at in its life cycle. During those periods when the discrepancy between needs and resources is great, kinship links, and also those of neighbourliness, are utilized in mobilizing labour services, which of course have to be reciprocated. A major difference however between Ashworthy and the urban districts is that in the former kinship is patri-centred. This is correlated with two circumstances; firstly, Ashworthy farm families own property inherited from father to son, while the urban families do not; secondly, in Ashworthy the father works at or near home, and the farmer, like the African peasant household head, is a small-scale entrepreneur using his wife and children as a labour team. Among urban families home and workplace are usually segregated, both spatially and as regards activities and personnel.

When Bethnal Green families moved to a new housing estate interaction with kinsfolk decreased, and also the companionable association with neighbours (friends of relatives, or relatives of friends) characteristic of that community. The nuclear family became much more individuated, and correlative with these changes the roles of husband and wife changed. In Bethnal Green the activities of husband and wife are different and separate, not only in that he is absent from home during working hours but also in that he spends his leisure in the pubs with other men, while she spends hers with female relatives and friends. In the new housing estate husband and wife carried out many activities together, and at different times each partner performed the same domestic tasks. In her study of conjugal roles entitled *Family and Social Network*, 1957, Elizabeth Bott explains how these different kinds of family organization are linked with the different kinds of social network surrounding the couple. Where the network is close-knit, i.e., where those composing it interact with each other as well as with the family, conjugal-role relationships are segregated, as described for Bethnal Green. Where the network is loose-knit, conjugal-role relationships of the joint sort are found. The first kind of

105

situation seems from all accounts to be typical of rural communities and of long-established working-class areas where there is some continuity of population. The concept of network, it should be remarked, is by no means useful only in furthering our understanding of conjugal roles. It has been used to aid analysis of social situations in new urban settlements in Africa, particularly by A. L. Epstein in *Politics in an Urban African Community*, 1958.

We are accustomed to think of stratification in our society in terms of broad categories marked off from each other by some well defined index and which include the population of the whole nation; for example, categories such as bourgeoisie and proletariat, or the Registrar General's five social classes distinguished by degrees of occupational prestige. A finding that emerges from several community studies is that at the local level there exist systems of stratification which do not coincide with any of these national models. For example, W. M. Williams in *The Sociology of an English Village: Gosforth*, 1956, describes how the population of Gosforth is divided, in the eyes of parishioners themselves, into seven status-groups distinguished by criteria not taken account of in the national models. For example, the difference between the top and second top strata is not one of wealth or occupation, since members of the latter can be richer than members of the former, but that members of the former behave 'like gentlemen' while the latter do not. The stereotype of the gentleman is a complicated one but includes such elements as distinguished descent, public school education, and connection with nationally prestigious institutions or persons. Ideally, Williams remarks, an individual could remain in the top stratum even if his financial position were of the lowest standard. At the bottom of the scale the lowest status group is also marked off from the one above it by behaviour and life-style, not by difference in occupation or wealth. The general nature of this life style is briefly indicated by the terms in which other groups describe them—'roughs and toughs', or 'people who don't try to lift themselves'. A distinction between *roughs* and *respectables* among the working class has been reported in many milieu studies; the latter

106

accept the middle-class norms in terms of which they themselves are not middle class, attempt to imitate them, spend money on home furnishings and their children, while the former reject middle-class norms and spend their money on immediate pleasures such as drinking and gambling.

Local status systems are important, however, not merely because the various status groups display different life styles, but also because the system structures relationships in a great many areas of life, particularly as regards leadership or direction of local voluntary associations such as the British Legion or the Angling Club. There are some two dozen of these, and despite the fact that the upper class form only six per cent of the total population, members of it occupy more than half of the positions of president and chairman in them. In general, status within the village organizations tends to reflect the status system within the community generally. In *Westrigg*, 1963, James Littlejohn describes how the local status system structures friendships and choice of marriage partner, friends and marriage partners being in the majority of cases status equals.

An interesting hypothesis has been advanced by R. Frankenberg in *Village on the Border*, 1965, to explain why members of voluntary associations composed of 'lower-class' persons so often elect 'upper-class' persons as leaders. The lower-class persons are divided into factions over disputes which often have nothing to do with the overt purposes of the association. At the same time, as fellow-villagers, they have to continue associating with each other in a wide variety of contexts, including everyday sociability. Quarrels must not become overt. Associations are used for the prosecution of covert disputes in this way; a proposal coming from one faction will be sabotaged by the opposing faction in such a way as to make it appear that responsibility for the check lies with the chairman. Hence they elect as chairman someone who is a 'stranger', someone not involved in the networks of relations by which faction support is mobilized and to whom responsibility for failure can be imputed without factional hostility being both publicly affirmed and exacerbated. An 'upper-class person' is in the position of 'stranger' to 'lower-class persons', hence is an eminently suitable candidate for chairmanship.

Since the local community in our society is embedded in the context of nation-wide economic and political systems, most students of it have at some point in their study to adopt Arensberg's first perspective and consider the community as object, attempt to separate out the characteristics of the community as a specific social formation from the phenomena within it, which are local reflections of the operations of the nation-wide systems. In *Westrigg,* the author describes how the processes of industrialization, urbanization and bureaucratization have in the present century transformed a remote rural community on the borders of Scotland. The abolition of the Parish Council and the School Board has deprived the parish of such administrative autonomy as it once had and curtailed to some extent the power of the local 'dominant class', the larger farmers. The local division of labour has been simplified, village craftsmen such as the smith or bootmaker being unable to compete with industrial production. The farms there are large-scale business enterprises each employing a variety of agricultural workers. Formerly they were 'servants', their working hours determined by the 'master' and paid not wages, but in farm produce and rights to graze sheep. Money wages have now replaced these, and membership of nation-wide unions mediates the relation between farmer and farm-workers. Farm organization resembles that of small industrial firms, in which the normal conflict between employer and employees is apparent, though softened by the rather more personal relation between farmers and workmen. Money wages, stipulated leisure time and better systems of transport have brought parishioners into closer contact with towns; they no longer have to live their lives solely with each other. The weakened integration of the community is reflected in the disappearance of institutions which both expressed and promoted it, such as neighbourly mutual aid or the sheep-shearing band, while the church, once the focus of local unity, no longer commands the loyalty of parishioners.

Yet the relation between the locality and the nation is

extremely complicated. A most illuminating study of it is given in Margaret Stacey's *Tradition and Change,* 1960, dealing with the small (pop. 19,000) town of Banbury in Oxfordshire. It is both an agricultural market and industrial manufacturing town. The features of community organization discussed above are of course present, but in addition a major cleavage is that between 'cosmopolitans' and 'locals'. Locals are those oriented to the local traditional social system, while cosmopolitans are those who, while having to reside and work in Banbury, yet reject or ignore the local system and derive their social frame of reference from organizations stretching beyond the locality. The distinction is not one between natives and non-natives, though many cosmopolitans are in fact recent immigrants to the town, nor is it one between status groups. Each in fact, has its own model of what the status system is. For example, locals regard as the top-class families who have for generations been dominant landowners and taken a prominent part in local government. These families are Anglican in religion and Conservative in politics and their children are educated in famous public schools. On the other hand, to the cosmopolitans Lord A. epitomizes the member of the highest class. He is chairman of several engineering companies, made his own way in the world and inhabits it rather than Banbury; though he owns a Hall in the district he seldom resides in it but commutes among the capitals of the world. He has no roots in the district and plays no part in local affairs. Different criteria apply at all levels of the two parallel models. A typical middle-class local owns a small family business, inherited from his father, considers public service a duty and is Anglican and Tory. His cosmopolitan equivalent has a degree from a provincial university and is a technologist in the aluminium factory. He is not much interested in religion, but joins local sports clubs. His main interest, however, is his own career, and he is ready to leave Banbury should his firm promote him elsewhere. A typical working-class local is employed in one of the small family firms, accepts the local status system, votes Conservative and belongs to no trade union. His cosmopolitan equivalent works in one of the

109

new large firms, belongs to a union and votes Labour. He does not accept the validity of the local status model, but considers that society is divided into simply bosses and workers. The significance of the cleavage is that it complicates social ties as compared with those described for example for Ashworthy. Members of the same class are liable to differ as to the purposes of local associations, or on policies for local government, but as they still have to get along with each other in work and daily-life antagonisms have to be muted.

Several other studies have reported a similar clash between traditional and non-traditional values. G. D. Mitchell, in an analysis of a district in South Devon (*Public Administration,* 1951), describes how until recently community leaders were mostly landed gentlemen and parsons whose authority was based on a belief in the sanctity of tradition. Despite recent attempts to base local authority in elected parish councils people eligible and suitable for election do not put themselves forward as candidates, on the ground that they are not the 'right people' to act as leaders. Doubtless in this area there are few cosmopolitans.

Recently in *Communities in Britain,* 1966, R. Frankenberg has attempted to provide a theoretical framework for the study of modern communities, based on researches mentioned above and several others. It is however, too complicated to summarize and can only be recommended to the reader as the best book to date on the subject.

SUGGESTED READING

FIRTH, R., *Elements of Social Organisation* (Watts, 1951).

FORTUNE, R. F., *Sorcerers of Dobu* (Routledge & Kegan Paul, revised edition, 1963).

NADEL, S. F. *A Black Byzantium* (Oxford University Press, 1942).

FEI, HSIAO-TUNG, *Peasant Life in China* (Routledge & Kegan Paul, 1939).

WILLIAMS, W., *A West Country Village: Ashworthy* (Routledge & Kegan Paul, 1963).

LITTLEJOHN, J., *Westrigg* (Routledge & Kegan Paul, 1963).

YOUNG, M., and WILLMOTT, P., *Family and Kinship in East London* (Penguin Books, 1957).

STACEY, M., *Tradition and Change* (Oxford University Press, 1960).

FRANKENBERG, R., *Communities in Britain* (Penguin Books, 1966).

MITCHELL, G. DUNCAN, 'The Parish Council and the Rural Community' in *Public Administration*, Winter 1951.

5

Small Groups

David M. Barkla

Introduction

Every human being is a member of some small groups and is forced to take an interest in them, in order to carry out his responsibilities to them and claim his rights from them. He needs to understand at least a little about how they work and how they act when things go wrong. He may well try to go further and seek to anticipate and prevent things going wrong in the groups of which he is a member. It is obviously reasonable for him to make these efforts, especially in a world in which things go wrong so often, but that is not at all the same thing as trying to understand small groups *in general*. It does not occur to most people to generalize even within the handful of groups of which they are members, still less from all the others. And why should they? Isn't it obvious that small groups differ enormously from each other? How, for instance, could we possibly expect to understand families better by studying groups of men at work or children at play? The main aim of this chapter is to begin to answer those objections, first by pointing out some features that all small groups have in common (but certainly not trying to deny their differences) and then by indicating some of the ways in which social scientists have actually tried to study small groups.

Different Kinds of Group

Group is not a very specific word; all it tells us is that more than one object is referred to, and that these objects form some kind of unity. It may be a unity only in the mind of somebody outside the group; for instance, I can think of the group which consists of 'the things lying on my desk', but when we think of groups of human beings most of the examples that spring to mind are also groups in the minds of their members. Usually, in a family, or a school class, or a club, or a team, or a committee, or a trade union, or a state, or a religious denomination, the members know they are members. They agree (more or less) about the nature of the group, and they have contacts with some or all of the other members in order to carry out the purposes of the group. But we ought to notice in passing that we can also think quite easily about groups that exist only in our own minds, for example the aged, or the poor, or the rich, or foreigners. These groups have no sort of existence outside our own minds until we define them unambiguously, and announce our definition to other interested people, but even if we do that (for instance by defining the aged as everybody over sixty-five) the members themselves might not agree that they constitute a group, and even if they agree that they constitute a group they might not have any contact with each other as a group. It is quite reasonable to talk about them as a group if we can define their membership and if their lives have something in common and different from other people's, but they are a conceptual group, not a real group, unless they deliberately make themselves into a real group. Conceptual groups and real groups are both interesting, but in different ways. In this chapter we are only concerned with real groups.

Even when he is dealing with the real groups, the primary task of the social scientist is not to find out and report what really happened in such-and-such a group at such-and-such a place and time. That is important, but it is the job of the journalist and the historian. The sociologist's job is to make generalizations about social behaviour and then to test them. There are several quite different ways of doing this with real groups. For instance, we can think of particular classes of real groups, such as families or professional associations, and

try to discover regular features of their historical development or their interaction with other sorts of group. Or we
can think of social processes such as education or law enforcement, and try to discover how different sorts of real
group mediate them; a comparison of selective schools with
comprehensive schools would be a study of this kind.

However, there is a quite different approach. Instead of
thinking about particular sorts of group we can think of real
groups as a class. We have already said that the only thing
they have in common is that their members have some sort of
deliberate contact with each other to fulfil the purposes of
the group. To study this sort of thing is to study organization.
The general question is: what determines the choice of procedures and rules in a group, and what effects do different
procedures and rules have on the life of the group? You may
feel this is a ridiculously broad question and that it all
depends on the circumstances of the group. But many people
make generalizations such as 'all groups need a strong leader'
or 'disputes in a group can usually be traced to faulty communications'. Right or wrong, these generalizations are interesting and important and so are worth studying.

Small Groups and Organizations

When we consider the whole range of possible groups from,
say, a courting couple to, say, the United Nations Organization, we can see that it is a formidable task to study their
organization, but we can divide them into two sets. There are
groups in which the members all meet face-to-face to consider and decide on the group's actions in some, if not all,
important matters, and there are groups in which the members never all meet in this way. A conjugal group of man
and wife or the committee of a youth club are clearly face-
to-face groups, and the R.A.F. or a political party are clearly
not face-to-face groups. The groups that do not meet face
to face have acquired the general title *organizations* and
they run their affairs through face-to-face groups which are
often referred to as *the management*. We are quite used to
these terms in this context, but that sometimes leads us to

114

assume quite wrongly that face-to-face groups are not organizations and do not need management, or that management is the concern only of people called 'managers'.

There is no fixed set of words for naming face-to-face
groups or their patterns of organization. Their distinguishing
feature is that their members interact as individuals with one
another in the group, hence the name 'face-to-face'. Such
groups are always small, ranging from two members to a
maximum which varies according to the exact nature of the
group, but is rarely more than fifteen; whereas an organization may have thousands of members. So *small groups* is a
convenient alternative description for face-to-face groups,
and is more often used. There is a third name, *primary
groups,* which is given because so many small groups are of
vital importance in the development of individuals (for example, parents and child, brothers and sisters, teacher and
pupil, boss and subordinate, friends), and because most social
action originates in small groups.

Some large groups, such as the House of Commons, meet all
together to conduct important business, but their members
are not expected to interact with each other as individuals
in the course of such meetings, and the group makes rules
to ensure that they do not. But of course, their members may
interact in various small groups outside the formal sessions,
and two individuals may know each other as members of
several different groups. There is no absolute boundary between small groups and organizations in terms of size, so it
can sometimes happen that a group changes from one state
to the other without altering its membership at all. Whenever that happens the members feel they have entered a new
world. (You see a glimpse of this in the change of atmosphere
in a school class when a teacher goes out of it.) There is a
profound difference of quality between small groups and
organizations; they have different possibilities and limitations in reality, and they are even more different in the
minds of their members. It is easy to understand why many
people feel that small groups are 'more real' than organizations; in a small group the whole thing is before our eyes,
and we do not feel so befogged by formalities. We can

bring far more of our personal resources to bear in our contacts with other members than we can in organizations. Some people go further and conclude that organizations—'bureaucracies'—are morally inferior to small groups, and should be abolished or avoided as far as possible. But the warm, rich intimacy of life in a small group produces a heavy crop of hatred, bullying, deceit, evasion and negligence. It needs sensitivity, courage and perseverance to act constructively and humanely in a small group, just the same qualities as it needs in an organization. We cannot say objectively that good work is more likely to be achieved in small groups than it is in organizations. But we cannot deny that people find small groups more exciting.

What Happens in Small Groups

You may think we have whittled down our subject very drastically by confining our interest to the organization of groups that are *not* 'organizations'; but worse is to come. There are some small groups, such as committees, or string quartets, or bridge partners, whose affairs are apparently dominated by quite clear rules and procedures. But we shall not concern ourselves with those sorts of rule or procedure. While they are in use the group has suspended its characteristic procedures; communication is no longer face-to-face but 'through the chair', or restricted in some analogous way, so that we can think of the group as having turned itself temporarily into a formal organization. For similar reasons we need not concern ourselves much with the technical tasks undertaken by the group. While the group's members are simply getting on with their jobs, whatever they may be, we cannot learn very much of the group's dynamics; at such times the group is in a relatively steady state. It is only when members interact with each other in such manner that their current practice is reinforced or weakened that we can begin to see the group's real potentialities and limitations.

That is not to say that all groups are equivalent, or that their particular tasks are unimportant to them. On the contrary, the interaction between members depends heavily on what the tasks are. However, the success or failure of the group to perform those tasks depends as much on the quality of the interaction itself as on the nature of the tasks. To put it another way, interaction itself *is* one of the main tasks in every group.

Interaction is an important task because it is the means of managing the group's activities. It becomes necessary when a group can no longer take its situation altogether for granted, and that happens from time to time in all groups (more often in some than in others) either because something unexpected happens to the group or because some disagreement emerges within the group about what should be done. So management entails:

1. watching for signs that something new and important to the group is happening (inside or outside the group) and diagnosing the change correctly;
2. producing proposals to deal with the new situation effectively;
3. deciding realistically between the proposals put forward. (Then starting again at No 1, to check the effects of the decision!)

None of these elements of management is easy or certain, and so we find that a great deal of actual interaction consists of more or less subtle devices for evading the real work. Of course, any such evasion is bad for the group in the long run, but the real work of management is rather daunting. It is to maintain progress along a knife-edge path through time, balanced between coping with immediate problems and preparing for the more distant and shadowy future, and balanced also between the diverse needs, aims and capacities of the different members of the group. This last point is vital. The members of a small face-to-face group have to put a lot of themselves into it if the group is to survive, and they can only do that if they get some substantial personal satisfaction out of it. Unfortunately, human beings have an extraordinary capacity for squeezing themselves into imaginary straitjackets, and getting substantial, though perverse, personal satisfaction out of the act, so we cannot assume that

117

a happy group is an efficient group. For example, it is very common for the members of a group to agree tacitly that some are 'natural' leaders and some are 'natural' followers; what that usually means is that some members are more assertive than others, but the assertive ones are not actually likely to be best at the first and third management tasks—diagnosis and realistic decision.

To take account of individual members' needs, aims, and capacities does not mean allowing each member to continue as he began in the group. He began inevitably on assumptions derived from his previous experience in other groups, and that could never provide an adequate understanding of the new group. Besides, he may never have explored his own position in previous groups; and again, his position changes as he grows and learns and ages. So it is an essential part of the work of management in a small group to find out and respond to what is going on inside the members themselves. Their changing position in the group, and in particular how they feel about themselves and each other, are important parts of the situation that the group has to manage. It is often said that 'personalities' interfere with the work of groups, and so they often do, but it is quite wrong to conclude that the group should keep 'personalities' out of its work. Personalities cannot be excluded; the group may deal with them well or badly, but it always has to deal with them somehow.

We can confirm this by a very simple analysis of the actual items of communication in any small group. Some of them are quite obviously about the group's task: questions, statements of fact, assessments of the situation, such as :

A. Have we enough for next year's running expenses?
B. We have £24 on current account and £200 on deposit.
C. But I expect typing will cost more next year.

But other communications seem quite irrelevant to the task, such as:

D. That was a gorgeous typist the agency sent last time.
E. She kept spilling my coffee in the saucer.
F. Some of us have to go and get our own coffee—in paper cups.

118

And others, although not altogether irrelevant, carry some extraneous meanings as well, such as:

- G. I've got something better to do than sit here waffling, even if you haven't.
- H. I've always said we ought to charge more for the annual dinner to build up our funds.
- J. Right, that's enough about finance. What's the next item?

(G. may be bringing the group back to the point, but he is also showing contempt. H. may have a valuable suggestion, but he stops short of actually making it, and even reminds the group that it has been rejected previously. J. may be exercising control, but he has omitted to make any decision on the matter in hand.)

Now, D., E. and F. have done nothing to advance the discussion, but they have provided the group with little bits of information about themselves. We must recognize that they are only little bits. We can and do build images of D., E. and F. even on such slender evidence as a written report of one of their remarks, but we are intuitively aware that the image would be stronger if we knew how D., E. and F. looked and sounded when they spoke. We know very well that a good deal of this type of communication is conveyed by catching somebody's eye, biting one's lip, fidgeting and so on, and by more automatic means like blushing or an altered rhythm of breathing. We are not so good at remembering that the meaning of a communication depends not only on the familiar habits of expression of the communicator, but also on the situation the group is in. People are inclined to say, for example, 'D. is always going on about girls', but that is of course an exaggeration, and it diverts them from observing what sorts of situation elicit such remarks from D. As long as D. remains one of the group's resources we can expect the group to gain from knowing when D. is likely to be side-tracked and when he is not.

The contributions of G., H. and J. present a more direct problem to the group. These three are not merely ignoring the group's task—they are positively adding to it in various

ways. For instance, the group must either accept G.'s implication that he is the only member whose time is important,
or they must reject it. Either way they will have to do something about it. They may appear to ignore it completely, but
that would in fact be a rejection of the implication, coupled
with an 'invitation' to G. to leave the group.

We should not assume that A., B. and C. do not inflict
their personalities on others. Perhaps, for instance, B. is so
mean that he won't give an opinion when asked for one, and
perhaps C. always expects everything to get worse. We must
also remember that this is only a single incident. It suggests
many questions, but we would need to observe many more
incidents before we could offer a reliable description of the
group, even in everyday terms.

Nevertheless, there are two points that are quite clear.
The first is that some at least of the members do have
personal feelings about the group or its present situation, and
some of them show signs of their feelings in what they say.
The second point is that no member has made any attempt
to report an observation of any of these feelings or ask a
question about them, still less to offer a diagnosis of them, or
a proposal concerned with them. In other words there has
been no attempt to apply the operations of management to
the problems foreshadowed by these expressions of feeling.
This is so common that we would have been disconcerted if
anybody in the group *had* drawn attention to his own or
another member's feelings. Members of groups can usually
persuade themselves that the personal feelings in the group
are unimportant, or that they will sort themselves out, or
that it is impossible to do anything about them, or that
doing anything would be an improper interference with
individual privacy. It is particularly noticeable that even in
groups devoted to the personal development of their members, such as families and groups of friends, members often
find it intolerably difficult to examine or deal with feelings.
It can be difficult even when the feelings themselves are
freely expressed and obviously important. The statement
'I'm completely fed up with the way you behave' is rarely

120

taken, or meant, as an offer of useful information about the speaker.

It is possible for the members of a group to collaborate to 'manage' their personal involvements in the group, but it is not often done comprehensively or persistently. It takes a lot of time and is often difficult and sometimes painful, so most groups make only sporadic and clumsy attempts at it. But if management is shirked the only possible alternative is inefficiency. Chronic inefficiency is 'normal' but acute inefficiency can lead to the breakdown of the group. The groups that take management most seriously are therapeutic groups, whose members have already suffered catastrophic breakdowns of relationships in other groups.

To sum up, management is one of the most fundamental aspects of group life and we can ask, about any communication in any small group: is this an attempt at management, or is it an expression of feeling, or is it a combination of the two? We can then go on to examine its effects in various ways; attempts at management are not always constructive, and expressions of feeling are not always destructive.

There are also other ways in which small groups are alike. They have a fairly clear beginning and ending in time. Since they depend essentially on the mutual interaction of particular individuals, it is a major event if one member leaves or if one enters, and if several people enter or leave a small group it is no longer the same group. So all small groups have to weld themselves into some sort of unity at the outset, and cope somehow with an inevitable dissolution.

All small groups spend a good deal of energy trying to protect themselves from change, at least after the original upheaval of establishing themselves as a group. They may not be able to control the external environment very well, but the members can do much to stabilize themselves internally by taking on particular specialized tasks, not only in operation, such as treasurer or tea-boy, but also in interaction, such as decision-maker, ideas man, rememberer of precedents, pointer-out of snags, and so on. They may also try to consolidate their identity by ruminating over their past exploits as a group, or by building up a fund of characteristics of their group in contrast to others. (The contrast may not be in favour of their own group; in fact one of the commonest myths within a group is that no other group is so unsatisfactory.) This sort of stabilization is not altogether satisfying to the group; members feel restricted by their own roles, and critical of the performance of other members in theirs.

When the accepted set of roles in the group becomes obviously inadequate, the group has to do something. It may move people from one role to another, which is a rather dramatic course usually involving open statements of dissatisfaction with particular members; or the group may redistribute the work without admitting it (perhaps even without realizing it), which leads to confusion and dishonesty; or it may call into question the assumptions on which roles are allocated, which is an attempt to manage the situation. In any case the group that has roles is sooner or later likely to have a crisis about them. The 'leadership crisis' is the most familiar, but there are potential crises relating to any other roles as well. Even while roles are acceptably filled the group has to contain them actively. Leaders have to be influenced as well as followed, sick members have to be carried as well as pitied, and wild members have to be restrained as well as envied. From the point of view of the person taking the role there is a continual conflict in what he wants from the others. He needs recognition and support for his role from the other members, and he needs recognition and support as a person; that is, somebody who carries potential not usable within the role. It is no wonder that people feel they are misunderstood by their wife or husband, parents, children, bosses, subordinates, teachers, or pupils; all these are strongly conventional roles, and it is difficult for others in the group to see through them to the person's other potential.

Because its individual members must belong to other groups as well, every small group has uncertainties about its boundaries. These uncertainties show themselves in concern about the loyalty of members to the group and to each other. How far can members be trusted to maintain the group's standards, or to keep the group's affairs confidential, or to refrain from using the group's resources for the benefit of competitive groups? This last can be a very pervasive and exhausting worry since *all* groups can be seen as competitors for one vitally important resource—members' time. The final stage of the concern is worry about the possibility of defection from the group. Every aspect of this problem is exacerbated when members of the group reduce the time they spend at its meetings, hence for instance the millions of hours spent in arguments about what time teenagers ought to come home.

Lastly, every small group has to deal directly with other small groups, that is, group to group and not merely because of overlapping membership. Groups in interaction act in many different ways, but almost always their behaviour towards each other is far more primitive, uncontrolled and inefficient than it is within the groups. It is as if the work they have done to make themselves into effective groups has taught them nothing about groups in general; they have to make all the old mistakes over again. It is one of the penalties of increasing the rate of social change that you thereby increase the rate of formation and interaction of new groups. It may even turn out to set an absolute limit to the rate of change obtainable, but that is at present a mere speculation.

All these universal aspects of small groups are ones which can be recognized easily enough by the members of groups, and sometimes are. Some of the categories used may be surprising at first but they are easy enough to apply to any actual group. They involve little more theoretical effort than the recognition that no group is exempted by its uniqueness from liability to universal problems. But we should notice that the common custom of ascribing actions, purposes and feelings to the group itself can conceal a number of different theoretical and empirical assumptions. When we say 'the group is relaxed' or 'the group is rejecting a member's contribution' we need not mean that the group has a will of its own, separate from the wills of its members, though some people do seem to mean that. We may merely be describing in simple words a complex process in which individual members interact to produce a consensus that suppresses hesitations, doubts and disagreements.

We can refine our description of events in a group in many ways and discover regularities that are not usually noticed, by classifying and counting particular sequences of events. When we do that we are beginning to explore divergences between groups rather than common features. All groups have problems about authority but some tend to tackle them by quarrelling, some by passive resistance, some by pretending the problems do not exist, and so on. There are many sources of diversity between groups, including, of course, the nature of their task. But some of the main sources are in the structure of the group and its composition. A group of two people has very different possibilities and limitations from those of any larger group, but each different number of members up to about seven introduces distinct new possibilities of specialization and of forming sub-groups and coalitions. These may be added to when there are differences of sex, age, race, language, profession and so on among the members. The combinations of all these factors are innumerable and there is no possibility of making a definitive typology of them; what is an important line of division in one group may go quite unnoticed in another, partly because homogeneous groups have to differentiate themselves, and heterogeneous groups have to coalesce, in order to get anything done at all.

Groups also differ in the span of their existence and the frequency and duration of their meetings; a discussion group may last only a few weeks, meeting for an hour a week, and a marriage may last over fifty years, with meetings lasting several hours every day. Obviously the opportunities for collaboration and development differ, but the groups do not necessarily differ in proportion to their opportunities. A group that sees plenty of time ahead tends to slacken its pace.

But some of the most obvious and important differences between groups seem to arise out of their own history, and to remain as persistent effects and causes of the group's failure or success. We often see a lively group, or an apathetic one, or a pompous one, or a decisive one, or an outward-looking one, or a bickering one, and as time goes on we hear repeated though perhaps oblique references to early incidents in its life, when its characteristic outlook and mode of interaction were 'laid down'. We may object that those early incidents themselves had antecedents in the previous experiences of members before they joined this group. But we cannot base very much on that, since we know that individuals behave differently in the different groups they belong to. It seems almost as though small groups are as tightly bound to their own past as individuals are to theirs.

Social Science and Small Groups

During the last hundred years or so, people who wanted to study human behaviour scientifically have usually gravitated to one or other of two main academic traditions: sociology (including anthropology) or psychology. There are other scientific traditions concerned with human affairs, such as economics, but they are more specialized; they deliberately exclude consideration of large sectors of life. Sociologists and psychologists like to think of their subjects as 'disciplines', that is, as having firmly established spheres of interest and methods of study, and although our successes have been limited and piecemeal the two subjects have at least acquired distinctive points of view. Neither of them really takes much account of groups, but both have provided useful new perspectives on groups.

The point of view of sociology will be apparent from other chapters in this book. It is enough to say here that the focus of sociologists' interest is society itself, and the ways in which social institutions and processes affect each other; in other words, sociologists regard societies as orderly systems, whatever disagreements they may have about the precise nature of the systems. Their aim is to discover rules that apply to whole groups in interaction with others, and that does not fit easily with a study of the internal workings of a group. For example, if we want to know whether there is a connection between the social class of schoolchildren and the extent of their involvement with school activities it will only confuse the issue if we study how children in particular schools interact. Whatever refinements we make to the question about social class and involvement in school, the 'small group' question of how the involvement is brought about remains a separate issue. Even when sociologists describe individual acts in social situations (which they often do, either as results of surveys or as an intuitive 'understanding' of the situation) they regard the individuals concerned as representatives of social roles. Yet in a sense the whole point of studying small groups is that people in groups do *not* behave strictly according to the requirements of their social roles. Nevertheless, as we shall see, sociologists have made a vitally important contribution to the study of small groups.

The reason for this odd state of affairs lies in the peculiarities of the other general behavioural science—psychology. The traditional point of view of psychology is that its natural unit of study is the individual human or other animal. That emphasis was already dominant in the psychology of philosophers who were interested in the structure of the mind, and in the psychology of psychiatrists who were interested in the treatment of mental illness. Whatever disputes there were about either, it was generally agreed that both the mind and mental illness were located inside individuals. The early development of scientific psychology, from about 1870 to about 1940, reinforced this emphasis; the search for laws of perception, learning and motivation was an attempt to discover the behavioural characteristics of a species, just as anatomists attempted to discover its structural characteristics. The notion of a species tended to imply the equivalence of its individual members, or at least their equivalence within statistically definable limits, and that implied that you could study *a* man, or a statistically adequate sample of men, as a way of studying *man*. (A statistical sample is the very opposite of a real group, because it has to be constituted in such a way that its members are not influenced by each other's membership at all.)

126

This was a quite deliberate attempt to turn psychology into a branch of biology, and many psychologists saw it as a programme of reducing psychology to physiological terms; some still do. This aim was attractive since it followed the enormously successful precedents of the natural sciences, and it did achieve notable success in some respects, such as the discoveries by Pavlov and other workers about the apparently automatic processes of conditioning, and the gradual unfolding of the complex processes mediating perception, which showed that the incredibly fine structures of our sense organs must be matched by equally fine and much more baffling structures inside our brains. So it was natural to think that the most interesting and important aspects of behaviour lay inside a creature, and behaviour between creatures was neglected, though not abandoned completely. There were always psychologists working at the level of what people themselves regarded as significant human experience, but until the 1940s even these mostly concentrated on the experience of 'the individual'. But they took the first steps towards subsequent work on groups, from several different directions.

One of the clearest starting-points was in psychoanalysis, because the significant experience of the patient was, according to Freud, firmly rooted in his childhood relations within his family. Freud believed that these early relationships profoundly affected adult social life, so he saw *group psychology* in general as the outcome of family psychology. In his own work he was concerned with only one sort of actual group, himself and the patient, but later psychoanalysts have tried to make direct observations of families and other groups. The experience of small children seems to be primitive as well as fundamental, and in recent years there has been some collaboration with students of mothering, and other 'instinctive' group behaviour, in animals; for instance, comparisons of international aggression have been made, by K. Lorenz and others, with the territorial behaviour of some animal species, but they are still very debatable. However that may turn out, the fundamental contribution of psychoanalysis to the study of groups is the recognition that a great deal of behaviour is determined by primitive forces of which we are usually unaware (and often quite unwilling to admit), and which lead us into apparently irrational and often self-defeating acts.

Another approach came from the *Gestalt* psychologists, a much more diverse group than the psychoanalysts. Their fundamental contribution was to distinguish between the real *geographical* environment in which a creature lives and the *behavioural* environment which shapes its actions. This behavioural environment is thought of as a field of forces organized in part by the state of the creature itself. The creature is seen as a *source* of events in the world, not a mere responder to events imposed on it from outside, as Pavlovians and other behaviourists saw it. But it is almost impossible to give an accurate impression of these theoretical positions in a few words, and their relations were very intricate; some of the *Gestalt* psychologists were far keener to reduce behaviour to physiology than were some of the behaviourists. However, a clear move towards social psychology was made by Kurt Lewin, who developed a version of *Gestalt* psychology which he called field theory, concerned with the *life space,* consisting of a person and his behavioural environment. Objects in this environment are more or less heavily charged with positive (attracting) or negative (repelling) *valence* for the person, which lead him to move within the *life space.* Perhaps the most important feature of this way of looking at behaviour is that anything, including other people, could be an object in the life space, and the forces that could be studied were not confined to crude hunger, thirst, fear of pain and the like, which the behaviourists usually had to work with because of technical limitations. It was not strictly impossible for behaviourists to study social behaviour, but it was a *tour de force,* whereas to Lewin and his followers it was a natural step, and they took it.

A third important approach was of a different kind: the gradual development of techniques for 'measuring' more or less stable tendencies in individuals, such as intelligence, personality traits and attitudes. These techniques depend partly on statistical theory, partly on mathematical theories of measurement (since we have nothing so simple as a trigonometry, let alone a yardstick, for measuring behaviour), partly on the art of phrasing questions inoffensively but unequivocally, partly on the training and supervision of those who administer the questions. They enable a psychological investigation to go beyond the immediate limits of observation by drawing on a stock of other psychologists' findings analysed and systematized in the form of tests; so we can not only observe what a person does, but also estimate, in some respects, what sort of person he is in other situations.

Most of the social scientists who have tried to study small groups have been psychologists, and most of them have been guided by one or more of these three approaches. On the whole they have been concerned about the interactions of the group with individual members: such questions as the relationship between the satisfaction of members and the productivity of the group, the pressures exerted by a majority on a minority, and especially on a single deviant, the kinds of person chosen as leaders by groups (in terms of their personalities or in terms of the assumptions made about them by other members, on the basis of their appearance and manner), the sequences of interactions between particular pairs and other sub-groups, the treatment of weak members, and so on. Some of the psychoanalytic workers, notably W. R. Bion, have studied behaviour in groups, in which members collude with one another to 'force' particular members into expressing one or other of the possible primitive responses, and in which there is a continual conflict between these unreflecting impulsive acts and the equally fundamental need of the group to come to terms with reality and get its work done. One of the most interesting aspects of this is the difficulty groups have in achieving a realistic view of other groups.

These are not the only possible psychological approaches. Without any very strong theoretical preconceptions, one can study the changes in behaviour in groups exposed to stresses of various kinds, such as a rapid increase in the pace at which they have to work, or the loss of one or more members. Or one can arbitrarily impose rules about how members may communicate with each other, and observe their effects on the efficiency of the group, or on its creativity, or one can work out the constraints imposed by particular sizes of group and particular sorts of task on the possibilities of making and shifting alliances and manipulating the balance of power.

It is at this point that the sociological voice has to be raised to remind us that the very existence of the small group implies the need for a different level of analysis. The small group is a miniature social system (though not by any means a miniature society) with a continuing need to review its aims and its procedures, so as to cope with a changing outside world and differentiated internal functions and structure (if only in terms of differences between members' personalities); and what happens in the group does not make sense if the group is regarded purely as a means towards its members' ends. Each member's behaviour is influenced by his awareness that he is part of a social unit which, as long as it survives, has claims on him, distinct from the claims exerted by other members as individuals. This point is so crucial to the understanding of small-group behaviour that it justifies the inclusion of small-group study as a concern of sociology, even though not very many sociologists are engaged in it.

The small group is in fact a setting in which psychologists must take sociology seriously and sociologists must take psychology seriously if they are to understand, and still more if they are to offer useful advice about the work of management.

Opportunities and Methods of Studying Small Groups

It cannot be said too often that studying human behaviour entails responsibilities towards the persons studied. We cannot simply study what we choose, unless we are prepared either to deceive our subjects, or to put up with very incomplete and possibly unreliable information. It is often supposed that the sheer pursuit of knowledge is its own justification, but if we actually ask people to give us information so that we can extend the common fund of knowledge we shall not get very much, unless the people concerned were itching to tell somebody anyway. That quite often happens and when it does the responsibility we incur is usually fairly small. But it becomes a different matter if we want to observe events instead of just hearing people's reminiscences of events, and even more different if we want to influence events in order to see if our theories are sound. In that case we have to establish our good faith, and the commonest and easiest way of doing that is to stand in a known and accepted professional position, rendering a service. We may, as an alternative, demand information because we stand in authority, but then we shall get only what our informant thinks it is safe to tell us. So it is not surprising that most studies of natural small groups have been conducted with some sort of therapeutic intention or at least to help the group to become better at its job.

The main impetus for the work came from a great increase in the felt need for it, arising from the stresses of the Second World War and its consequences, and a more gradual increase in the readiness of professionals to treat groups rather than individuals. The need was apparent in the acute wartime problems of selecting leaders for military groups, maintaining the morale of groups and their productivity, helping servicemen who had 'broken down' to become re-integrated in military or civilian work groups, and so on. After the war, when technical innovations continued to flourish, and the future became increasing unpredictable in many ways, there arose additional problems about coping with resistance to technical and organizational changes, making training courses more effective, making psychotherapy available to more patients and, finally, educating people who had to work in groups to understand more about them. The response of professionals was aroused partly by the theoretical developments we have already mentioned, and the intrinsic interest of the work, and partly by the large and growing demand for help.

The opportunities thus offered for helping and studying groups have been of three kinds :

1. Where a professional helper is admitted into an existing

group as observer and adviser, for example, 'behavioural science consultants' working with groups of staff in organizations, or psychotherapists working with whole families. The helper has to remain on a different footing from the other members, but they may try hard to convert him into an ordinary member.

2. Where professional helpers establish special groups for people who live in different situations, but face similar problems of social interaction. This is group psychotherapy; it is done in many different ways, but it always includes a separate helper—the therapist—whose job is to confront the other members with their own behaviour seen from a different point of view, in order to give them new insight into it. Although the interaction of the members with each other is a vital element in the 'teaching' situation, the presence of the helper makes the process radically different from that in mutual-help groups such as Alcoholics Anonymous, where the beliefs and actions of the group as a whole are seldom in question.

3. Where professional helpers establish training groups (often called T-groups) for people whose work includes management of small groups. This resembles group psychotherapy in that participants are confronted with their own behaviour and encouraged to try new ways of coping with social situations in a safe setting, but as they are mostly not in acute personal difficulties, training is usually much briefer and less radical than therapy. Training tends to employ a variety of techniques for simulating different aspects of group relations in general, whereas therapy has to be more tightly linked to the particular problems of individual members.

The professional helper has relatively little control over a group to which he is brought as a consultant; he has more control over a group he has started as a therapist, and still more over a training group as a director of studies. So we might expect the training situation to be best for research, but unfortunately this sort of control tends to suppress some of the processes we are most interested in. Things do happen in training groups, but not quite like what happens in the groups the trainees are going to work in. There is always some distortion involved in using one type of group to simulate another type, and if we use a group protected by professional safeguards to simulate one whose members must sink or swim, the distortion may be great. It is most obvious when the protected group is one set up solely for an experiment, and its members have little to gain or lose from what they do in it. But scientific explanation requires systematic observation, and, since experiments are by far the most reliable and economical way of controlling observations, many social scientists are willing to put up with the uncertainties of interpreting their conclusions.

As well as logical and technical difficulties, experiments produce ethical problems. Applying different treatments to real groups is acceptable only if there is genuine doubt about which treatment is best for their members. That is one reason for setting up special experimental groups; then experimenters can 'pretend' to apply different treatments, removing any possible bad effects by assuring the group afterwards that the situation had not been what it seemed. This can be defended as the only practicable way to evaluate social techniques that might be either beneficial or harmful—but it may lead people to doubt whether they should ever believe what a social scientist says.

Experiments and other methods of control help us to avoid drawing unfounded conclusions from what we observe, but they are no use unless we do observe something important, and record it. Behaviour in human groups is often so fast, intricate and intense that observers find recording or remembering very difficult, but the task of analysing film or tape recordings, or even shorthand transcripts, is so heavy that it is often better to have a much cruder record, confined to what is expected to be most important. That brings in further possibilities of distortion because, although people rapidly get used to being observed and recorded, they are certainly influenced in their behaviour if they are aware that some things are recorded and others are not.

The outstanding problem of observing behaviour in human groups is that in any meeting of the group there are events whose causes lie in previous meetings or even in other groups. Most people make some use of obvious clues to the influence of the past, such as differences of age or sex among members, or generally recognized styles of clothing or speech. There are very diverse views about how much further one could hope to see into the origins of the group's behaviour. Some researchers treat the pasts of different members as sources of haphazard variations in present behaviour; some make an allowance for the past by categorizing members on the basis of personality tests; some watch for members to reveal unconsciously held (and therefore presumably deep-rooted) attitudes about one another. In any case, a researcher is making observations correctly if, and only if, they help him to make correct predictions. But since an event in a group may have different meanings for different members, and may indeed have several different levels of meaning for any individual, it can lead to several different sorts of correct prediction. There is no order of merit among levels of explanation or the research techniques associated with them, but it is difficult for a researcher to use more than one approach at a time. In practice researchers mostly come to specialize in the use of one approach rather than in the explication of one event. Then their friends say they are engaged in scholarly theory-building, and their enemies say they are engaged in academic empire-building.

We are still far from knowing everything about small groups. Fresh minds and careful study, coupled with luck, will sooner or later produce unexpected observations and novel theories, and perhaps—who knows?—vaster academic empires.

SUGGESTED READING

The literature on small groups is now very large indeed, but there are several small introductory books that are well worth reading, for instance:

MILLS, T. M., *The Sociology of Small Groups* (New Jersey: Prentice-Hall, 1967). An excellent general introduction containing a good reading list.

KLEIN, J., *Working with Groups* (Hutchinson, 1961). A very lucid account of some important methods.

RICHARDSON, E., *Group Study for Teachers* (Routledge & Kegan Paul, 1967). A clear description of an approach to small groups based on Bion's ideas and methods.

Some other books that are relevant

SCHEIN, E. H., *Organizational Psychology* (New Jersey: Prentice-Hall, 1965). This presents the fundamental issues of management in groups.

BION, W. R., *Experience in Groups* (Tavistock Publications, 1961). A classic, and rather more difficult than the others in this list.

There are very many paperbacks on psychotherapy in groups, and other particular types of group, but they are usually rather advanced, sometimes more than their titles suggest. There are also some good general introductions to social psychology, e.g. BROWN, R., *Social Psychology* (Glencoe, Illinois: Free Press, 1965). The main handbooks on small groups are:

HARE, A. P., BORGATTA, E. F. and BALES, R. F., *Small Groups* (New York: Knopf, 1955).

CARTWRIGHT, D., and ZANDER, A., *Group Dynamics: Research and Theory* (Tavistock Publications, third edition 1968).

BRADFORD, L. P., GIBB, J. R., and BENNE, K. D., *T-Group Theory and Laboratory Method* (New York: Knopf, 1964).

6

Social Deviance

Howard Jones

Social deviance is problem behaviour. It is the behaviour of those who 'kick over the traces', or opt out of social regulations. The study of social deviance is thus the study of non-conformists, and in particular of those non-conformists whom society sees as undesirables: its criminals, problem families, tramps, alcoholics, drug addicts, suicides, and also those whose neglect of social rules, though censured, is less seriously regarded, such as truants, cheats, and income-tax evaders.

Not all social problems are, of course, forms of deviance. Poverty, slum housing, and ill-health are all problems both for those who experience them and for any society which has set itself the task of providing a reasonable standard of life for its members, but no question of social non-conformity on anybody's part is necessarily involved. Nor, even in true forms of deviance, is the deviant's behaviour necessarily a problem to himself. Many would argue that but for the existence of the police and the penal system, the criminal would have no problems. Nevertheless, social deviance is a social problem in being a problem to society itself. And although his non-conforming behaviour may not be a problem to the deviant, the action a society takes in order to bring him into line often presents him with serious problems. Sometimes these enforcement measures represent real secondary social problems in themselves; no one who has ever witnessed the squalor and corruption of Her Majesty's local prisons can have any doubt about that.

It is the problem aspect of social deviance which attracts many sociologists to this field of study. They are social reformers and wish to find cures for social ills. So they would like to understand what makes a man a criminal or a suicide, an alcoholic or a feckless layabout with the aim of removing those causes and reducing the incidence of the deviant behaviour in question. It is easy enough to understand why philanthropically-minded social scientists should want to tackle such problems as poverty. No-one would dispute that the suffering which they carry with them is undesirable and ought to be eliminated. The case is somewhat different with social deviance. Here one is concerned with eliminating not poverty, but social non-conformity. It implies a degree of confidence in the superiority of conventional standards of behaviour, which is not necessarily shared by those whom one seeks to change.

For such reasons the reformist approach to social deviance is not accepted by all sociologists, especially those who consider that, as social scientists, they should adopt a degree of scientific detachment from the social arrangements which are the subject matter of their investigations. After all, the social rules which the deviant is rejecting are themselves part of that subject matter, and to identify with them as the reformers are said to do hardly makes for objectivity in studying them.

To the more scientifically-minded sociologists the study of social deviance is justified instead by the contribution which can be made to understanding the social rules themselves. Deviant behaviour represents a breach in the social consensus, and is thus of fundamental importance for the understanding of what makes and sustains a society. On this view the study of crime and other kinds of deviance is justified by the contribution it can make to the development of a corpus of basic theoretical knowledge about society, i.e., to the development of sociology itself.

Because sociologists themselves have been subjected to life-long processes of social indoctrination and have to live their lives as sociologists as well as citizens, within the same framework of social pressures as everybody else, there is clearly a

137

limit to the amount of scientific detachment which they can achieve in studying society. Their thirst for objectivity may be so strong as to blind them to the extent to which they are inescapably involved with their society. Where this happens, they may be in even more danger of falling prey to subjective bias than reformers who are aware of their involvement and are on guard against it. In the end the choice between these two positions probably depends more on the temperament and the social background of the sociologist himself, and particularly on the latter, than on anything else. There is a branch of sociology which examines the effect which society itself has upon the growth of knowledge, and there is no reason to believe that sociology itself is exempt from such influences.

In the years between the wars there was no doubt in the minds of those interested in deviance that it was a sign of something wrong. As against earlier views that it arose out of the moral defects of the deviant himself (that is, that he was a *bad* person who therefore committed *bad* acts), it was argued that he was himself a victim of either a bad environment or a very damaging upbringing. In other words there was a shift from seeing the deviant as wicked to seeing him as abnormal, and this led to an emphasis upon treatment rather than punishment. Incidentally, it was also a step towards a scientific approach to these problems, in that people came to see deviant behaviour as the result of causes rather than punishment. Incidentally, it was also a step debased free will of the individual himself.

For instance, it was noted that crime and other forms of problem behaviour were commonly associated with an underprivileged social position, such as living in slums, being poor or unemployed and having an inadequate education. Remove social injustice, and problem behaviour, if not actually eliminated, would be greatly reduced. Many social reformers were inspired by this belief, which played some part in providing a justification for the measures of social amelioration which swept away many of the slums in this country and eventually produced the structure of public social services which we have come to call the Welfare State. Nobody would suggest that poverty has been eliminated even now and deplorable housing conditions still persist in certain of our industrial cities. Nevertheless, many of these conditions have been improved, and as a result we are as a nation better off than we have ever been. It is a sad comment upon the idealism of many of our social reformers that, despite these improvements in our social conditions, social deviance is more extensive than it has ever been before. The following table gives some idea of the scale of the increase in criminality alone:

NUMBERS FOUND GUILTY OF INDICTABLE OFFENCES PER
100,000 OF POPULATION IN THE AGE GROUP

Years	Juveniles*	Adults
1953/57 (Annual average)	678	230
1958/62 (Annual average)	947	327
1963	1,068	414
1964	1,274	405
1965	1,342	439
1966	1,345	479
1967	1,342	503

*This refers to the age group 8 and under 17 until 1964,when the raising of the age of criminal responsibility meant using the age group 10 and under 17 from February 1964.

There are many precautions which have to be observed in interpreting statistics such as these. The most important is that they are rarely complete. There is usually a sizeable 'dark figure' which, for one reason or another, has never come to light. And of course variations in the dark figure between one year and another may give a false impression of the increase which has actually occurred over a period. Nevertheless, there seems no doubt that the improvement in social conditions in this country has been accompanied by an increase rather than a decrease in social deviance. This does not mean, of course, that social reform is necessarily a bad thing; it is presumably to be justified by the suffering which it relieves, and by the satisfaction of people's feelings of social justice. What is clear is that it cannot be justified by its effect in reducing anti-social behaviour.

The idea that a bad social environment produces bad citizens is a relatively unsophisticated theory, which can be shared by social scientists and lay social reformers alike. The psychiatric view of deviance which had its hey-day during and immediately after the Second World War called for more specialized knowledge. Although the idea that anti-social behaviour was connected with mental deficiency or serious forms of mental illness had been held for a long time, the more elaborate theories of the Freudians now put a completely fresh complexion upon the idea of a connection between psychological abnormality and social deviance. Freud himself had already described cases in which unconscious motives could lead not only to neurotic symptoms, but in certain cases to symptoms of a criminal character. Thus the emotionally disturbed person may commit criminal acts without knowing why, and under circumstances in which his behaviour seems very irrational to people not subject to the same inner compulsions. Among such a group would be found what Freud called the 'criminal from an unconscious sense of guilt', whose unrecognized feelings of remorse drive him to commit crimes in order to be punished and thus allay his guilt. As his aim is to be punished, he always somehow manages to be caught. For such a person legal punishment can have little deterrent force. Freud had also suggested that suicide was the result of the turning of an individual's normally outgoing aggression upon himself because of his own intense sense of guilt. In the main, states such as these were seen to be the result of faulty (usually deprived) upbringing by parents.

A further important contribution, especially to the psychopathology of criminality, came from August Aichhorn in a very influential book called *Wayward Youth,* 1925. Freud had distinguished between the *id,* the wish-fulfilling functions of the mind, which he saw as primitive and instinctual, and those restraints on his impulses which the individual imposes upon himself, as a result of the social training he receives within his family in childhood. These latter constituted what Freud called the *ego* (restraints based on 'reality' considerations) and the *super ego* (based on

140

morality). Aichhorn argued that criminal tendencies were due to a failure to incorporate an adequate ego and super ego within the criminal's psyche. Because a child is willing to give up his instinctual satisfactions only for those whom he loves, a deficiency in love in his early environment means that he fails to identify with his parents and impose on himself the sort of restraints which they wish him to learn. Thus he remains a pleasure-seeking creature, weak in both the sense of reality and moral sense, and so becomes a delinquent. Because of the more recent work of Dr John Bowlby,[1] a more fully-worked out version of Aichhorn's theory has become tremendously influential in ideas about the case of children since the war.

It is now generally accepted that lack of parental love in infancy is a major cause of abnormal development in later life, and may sometimes lead to deviant behaviour. On the other hand, unloving parents are themselves deviants of another kind. Often their failure to give sufficient emotional nurture to their children results from emotional difficulties from which they are themselves suffering, which may in their turn go back to their own deprived childhood. They are seen as no more free agents than their own children and as much in need of treatment. Simple advice to parents on how to bring up their children is therefore rarely seen as enough; a more subtle approach through casework or even psychotherapy is called for.

It would be impossible to list the names of all those who have contributed to the many psychological theories of deviance. It has been a very rich harvest indeed, ranging from the infant-training theories of Bowlby, to the work of H. J. Eysenck, who sees the problem of persistent criminality as primarily one of a congenital inability to learn social behaviour.[2] The psychological trend has now perhaps run its course. Attention has shifted back to the social environment, though perhaps in a less naïve fashion than in the past. It is no longer simply taken for granted that human beings need only a good environment to become good people. The possible connection between deviant behaviour and social conditions has been studied in more detail and in the light of the growing body of theory about the way in which society itself operates. In other words, the study of social deviance has been properly domesticated at last within the general field of sociological theory.

During the 1930s, the Chicago school of social ecologists, led by Clifford R. Shaw, had plotted the home addresses of juvenile delinquents, mental patients, and those dependent for financial support upon welfare agencies on a map of Chicago, and had shown that they tended to live in certain deteriorated neighbourhoods, forming a ring immediately around the 'bright lights' city centre. Although in other studies the actual location of these 'blighted areas' tended to vary, and although, in particular, slum clearance in Britain meant that high delinquency areas were often on new housing estates on the outskirts of our cities, the concentration of problem behaviour in certain localities seems unquestionable. Shaw and his collaborators tended, in accordance with the social reform climate of the time, to attribute problem behaviour to slum conditions, which its location on new housing estates refutes. Nevertheless they made an important point in suggesting that, in communities of this kind, what the residents of other localities might see as deviant behaviour is acceptable and even possibly essential if one is to be accepted by one's neighbours as *normal*. A tradition of delinquency develops and is then transmitted from one generation to another by the normal processes of social education. Thus seen from the standpoint of respectable society, it is not the individual who is deviant but the neighbourhood and culture within which he has grown up. To set out to change his behaviour without, at the same time, doing something about his social environment would be unrealistic. If it succeeded (which was highly unlikely) it would result in his being maladjusted to his own social setting.

The delinquent person, then, is normal. He has learned to adapt himself to his society only too well. One might nevertheless argue that his society is *sick,* in which case measures of rehabilitation would have to be directed towards it rather than towards him. This was the conclusion reached by the Chicago group, who set in train the Chicago Area

Projects to stimulate residents of these 'blighted areas' into tackling their own communal problems. Professional 'community social workers' would be employed, but solely with the aim of stimulating this process of self-discovery and self-help within the neighbourhood. Where previous psychological approaches to therapeutic treatment had emphasized changing individuals, the Chicago Area Projects took as their motto the phrase, *Change the street.*

The Chicago theory, that deviant behaviour was learned by a normal social process, needed to be systematized if it was to be subjected to empirical test. This task was performed by E. H. Sutherland with his theory of differential association.[3] Sutherland, who was mainly concerned with the explanation of criminal behaviour, argued that as we move about in society we are constantly hearing favourable and unfavourable attitudes expressed towards crime. He argued that if we encounter more definitions favourable to crime than unfavourable ones, we are likely to become criminal in our turn.

In its crudest form this theory is open to certain very severe objections. After all, few people meet more criminal definitions than the police, and on Sutherland's theory, they should therefore be a highly criminal group. Sutherland did, however, go on to argue that the force which definitions have for us depends upon their frequency, duration, priority (in time), and intensity. How often definitions are expressed and how long our exposure to them lasts, are obvious factors. Sutherland also suggests that priority is important in that earlier exposure is likely to be more influential than later experiences. Intensity may be the most important of all in determining how a definition affects those who encounter it. The question of how the police come to be influenced more by the anti-criminal than by the pro-criminal definitions which they meet in the course of their daily work, is probably just such a question of the relative weights which they attach to each.

In other words, the individual is not a mere passive recipient of impressions from his environment, but an active selector between those impressions. The important question which Sutherland did not ask himself is how we do come to accept certain of these influences and reject others. It may be by means of the application of the psychoanalytic theory of identification through an emotional bond, that further understanding of this will emerge.

A number of writers now argue that what the respectable classes see as deviant behaviour is the natural behaviour of the lower or *rough* working class in modern industrial societies. Because the conventional rules and laws of these societies are formulated in accordance with the standards and moral judgments of the socially dominant, respectable groups, this normal behaviour of the rough working class becomes deviant or criminal by definition. From this point of view, there is nothing intrinsically undesirable about their behaviour, given their own moral standpoint, which is more concerned with immediate gratification, and less with saving, planning and looking forward, than is that of the dominant group. However imprudent this may be, there is nothing morally reprehensible about it, and certainly not in the minds of the rough working class themselves.

The social learning theory of deviance has thus come a long way from the original idea of the social ecologists that deviant behaviour was a result of life in sick, 'blighted' neighbourhoods. Deviant behaviour is now seen as being transmitted from one generation to another within a culture dominated by others with more social power and whose standards are different. Such moral relativity makes it difficult to approach, say, the juvenile delinquent on a moral basis. You are asking him not simply to become good, or to try to 'cure himself', but to change sides, presenting him not only with a moral problem, but even more importantly with a practical problem of how to establish social relationships with his own people afterwards.

Many will still feel that some forms of deviant behaviour are undesirable in themselves. They point to the fact that criminals often feel the need to justify themselves; visitors to prisons often remark on the frequency with which prisoners deny having committed the crimes for which they have been sentenced. Why should they bother if they feel morally secure about their behaviour? G. M. Sykes and D. R. Matza argue that the crucial stage in the development of an offender is his learning, within his social setting, certain justifications which enable him to commit crimes without feeling guilty.

'I didn't mean it.' 'I didn't really hurt anybody.' 'They had it coming to them.' 'Everybody's picking on me.' 'I didn't do it for myself.' These slogans or their variants, we hypothesize, prepare the juvenile for delinquent acts. These 'definitions of the situation' represent tangential or glancing blows at the dominant normative system rather than the creation of an opposing ideology.[4]

An application of these ideas has come from D. R. Cressey,[5] who has shown how the embezzler, not being usually a professional criminal, needs before he can embezzle other people's money to be able to justify such behaviour to himself by some such rationalization as, 'I was borrowing, not stealing it'.

Possibly it is an over-simplification to assume that all criminals are defensive about their criminality in the way described by Sykes and Matza; or alternatively that all criminals are combatants in a subcultural conflict, and are happy and contented with their own insular morality. One probably has to take account of both kinds of criminals. As studies of social class have shown, there are members of the working class who aspire to membership of the middle class and others who do not.

The ideas of Sykes and Matza form a bridge to a second kind of sociological theory about deviance. Although they recognize that separate subcultures do exist, and indeed that it is within these subcultures that the deviant learns his rationalizations, they argue that his guilt about his deviant behaviour implies that there is a general acceptance throughout the society of certain basic values. In other words, although society is riven, this is not part of its essential nature, but a kind of aberration; a defect in its structure which leads to problem behaviour. Thus one has moved away from talking about individual emotional sickness as the cause of delinquency towards talking, in effect, about a sickness of

145

society itself. Ideas along these lines have been developed
most fully by *anomie* theorists starting from a concept
originally developed by the French sociologist, Emile Durkheim.

In his famous study, *Suicide,* Durkheim pointed to the
breakdown in social standards which occurs at times of rapid
social change. He had in mind, in particular, the rapid
improvement or deterioration in economic conditions, leading in either case to a breakdown in the established expectations of individuals about their standard of living and their
way of life. Deprived of the signposts in the shape of social
norms which the individual has relied upon in steering himself through life, he becomes lost and disorientated, and
destroys himself. As another example, Durkheim sees suicide
occurring in widowhood as due to domestic anomie: the
survivor cannot adjust herself to the new situation in which
she finds herself. Durkheim did not argue that all suicides
were caused by anomie. Some, called *altruistic* suicide, consisted of self-destruction enjoined upon the individual by
society itself. An example of this would be the institution of
suttee under which the widow of a Hindu was formerly
expected to throw herself on her husband's funeral pyre.
This is an example of behaviour arising from the positive
moral pressures of a subculture, which members of other
subcultures would see as deviant and undesirable. In this
respect it closely resembles the subcultural delinquency described above. Still another form Durkheim called *egoistic*
suicide, arising from isolation. It has been suggested, however, that egoistic suicide may be another aspect, as seen
through the feelings of the suicide himself, of anomic suicide.
The socially isolated person, the unmarried person, the
widowed, the Protestant (as compared with the Catholic)
are all in situations in which they do not have the support
of an integrated group with a strong framework of common
norms.

Nevertheless, some interesting and important applications
of the idea of social isolation as a cause of suicide have been
made, notably by A. F. Henry and J. F. Short.[6] They make
use of a widely accepted psychological generalization that,

other things being equal, increased frustration leads to an increase in aggressive behaviour on the part of human beings. Thus both homicide and suicide might be correlated with the amount of frustration which a society imposes on its members. Whether they express their aggression outwardly as homicide or inwardly as suicide is said to depend upon whether they can blame their frustration on other people, or can blame it only on themselves. A high degree of social involvement carrying with it many externally imposed restraints leads to the former possibility, and a high rate of homicide. A relatively isolated social situation, in which the individual's predicament can be blamed only upon himself leads to his aggression being directed inwards upon himself, and so to suicide. A second factor was social status: high status meant fewer external restraints and therefore more suicides and vice versa.

This is a most illuminating and elegant theory, explaining a good deal of the available data, but it is a psychological rather than a sociological approach to the problem. *Anomie,* focusing as it does upon the social structure, has attracted more attention from sociologists. Recent developments in *anomie* theory have been among the most important growing points not only for the understanding of deviance, but also for the development of sociological theory itself.

The basic assumption in many psychological approaches to the understanding of social behaviour is that there is a fundamental antagonism between the individual with his own selfish needs, and society which expects him to share with, and sometimes even to yield place to, others. Such an antagonism was implied in Freud's picture of the human infant as a bundle of primitive, animal instincts who has to be civilized through social training, often at the cost of doing violence to his instincts and in extreme cases producing severe unconscious conflicts in him and possibly neurotic symptoms. More recently, though in a very different form, the learning theorists with their ideas about social conditioning, have taken up a similar stance. Henry and Short, who see external relationships as sources of frustration, are in the same tradition. This viewpoint appears to be clearly at variance with that of Durkheim, who argues instead that the very lack of social norms leads to suicide. In fact, the difference between, say, Freud and Durkheim is possibly less than it appears at first sight. Freud recognized the existence of gregarious impulses of various kinds, and even gave the infant's dependence upon his mother priority over his more self-centred impulses, arguing that social training only occurred because the infant was prepared to restrain his selfish demands in order to retain her love. The view that social roles are essential if human beings are to be happy and stable lies at the very heart of the concept of *anomie*. An anomic society is a sick society in which those necessary rules are deficient in some way.

Following Durkheim's original formulation, the nature of those deficiencies has been more carefully examined by Robert K. Merton. Instead of talking simply about lack of norms he described a situation in which, although norms existed, they were inconsistent with one another. A society offers goals which well-adjusted members accept as their own and try to achieve. At the same time it offers socially approved channels through which these goals may be reached. In a monistic society, in which the same values are accepted by all classes and groups within the society, these goals and channels would be the same for everybody. All would seek to achieve the objectives which society has put before its members as desirable, and as a result all would attempt to take advantage of the channels available for their attainment. But because of differences in wealth, education and social contacts, not all do, in fact, have equal access to the approved channels. In particular, in modern America, the goal of success is widely accepted but members of the working class have relatively little chance of achieving it. In this intolerable personal conflict, working-class Americans are tempted to abandon the norms embodied either in the means, the ends, or both. Social norms have become virtually untenable; *anomie* has arrived by a new route.

Merton describes, for instance, the *innovator* who has learned the success goal too well to give it up, and finding himself unable to achieve it by legitimate means has set out to get there by another less respectable route. Merton suggested that this is a possible explanation of much crime. The *ritualist*, on the other hand, has given up the goal as unobtainable, gaining his sense of worthwhileness by performing all 'the right motions'. Having quenched his ambitions, he becomes a good citizen in the most conventional sense, doing all the right things; but for that very reason in his underprivileged position dooming himself to impotence. Apart from the *rebel*, who seeks to change both means and ends in a positive sense, Merton also describes another deviant solution in the form of the *retreatist* who gives up any attempt at a social solution, preferring to retreat from his *impasse* into personal fantasies of a wish-fulfilment kind, often with the aid of drugs or alcohol. The idea of the retreatist as the 'drop-out' has received a good deal of prominence in recent discussions of drug addiction.

Albert Cohen, harking back briefly to the work of the social ecologists, pointed out in his book, *Delinquent Boys*, 1956, that although they had established that a deviant tradition was transmitted from one generation to another through the normal processes of social learning within delinquency areas, they had provided no convincing explanation of how those norms arise in the first place. Cohen, primarily interested in the adolescent delinquent gangs which form in such areas, believed that the answer was to be found in a version of Merton's *anomie* theory, though a version having a more psychological flavour than that of Merton's. About to enter adult life, and therefore facing the dilemma represented for him by a society which does not live up to its pretensions, the working-class youth is in a painful personal dilemma. He solves this for himself through a 'sour grapes' formula in which he attacks what he really loves. He makes use of a mechanism which Freud called *reaction formation*, in which an individual who wants something very badly but cannot have it banishes the wish into his unconscious and then protects himself against its re-emergence, and his consequent discomforture, by asserting very loudly that it was the very last thing he really wanted. 'The lady doth protest too much,' said Shakespeare in *Hamlet*. Among working-class

149

young people, Cohen saw their protestations as taking the form of a violent attack upon that very middle-class respectability to which they had unsuccessfully aspired.

Cohen contended that such a theory accounted for the violent and destructive character of much teenage delinquency at the present time. Moreover, it showed that this violence was not as senseless as it might appear at first sight. Certainly it led to no material gain for the offenders, but it did serve to relieve their inner sense of frustration, i.e., the profit for them was emotional.

This viewpoint was strongly criticized by R. A. Cloward and L. E. Ohlin[7] who denied what had been taken for granted by both Merton and Cohen—that all members of a society did start out by accepting the same overall values. While some members of the working class did share the same goals, disseminated through society because of the control by the socially powerful middle class of the main organs of social education, and in particular through the schools. Despite this monopoly of the formal machinery of education, not all of the working class were won over. For them the norms derived from their informal relationships within their families and neighbourhoods were of more importance. A similar distinction has often been made in postwar community studies in this country between the *rough*, on the one hand, and the *respectable* or upward aspiring working-class, on the other. According to Cloward and Ohlin, the American middle class and the respectable working-class set before themselves objectives of both material success and a high-status way of life, but the rough working class set themselves a target expressed almost entirely in terms of material success. Both rough and respectable, however, would find their particular aims unrealizable. Both had internalized aims to which, as working-class people, they then had little or no access.

Attention thus shifts to the structure of opportunities in the communities within which people live. In an anomic situation people are deprived of adequate legitimate opportunities. But what of illegitimate opportunities? If a gang of adolescent vandals exists in one's neighbourhood, then there is here an illegitimate opportunity to adopt the kind of solution postulated by Albert Cohen. Cloward and Ohlin certainly see this as one of the results of the anomic disjunction between means and ends, but only for the upward-aspiring sections of the working class who have identified with middle-class standards and therefore need to denounce these standards to themselves and to others in order to be at peace within themselves.

Others become *innovators* in Merton's sense, seeking to achieve not middle-class status, but material success by any means which may be available to them. It is obvious that they could not hope to achieve middle-class respectability through dishonest behaviour, though it might well bring them material rewards. But they, too, need an appropriate local structure of illegitimate opportunities. If their ill-gotten gains are to lead to any sort of success in terms of their own lower working-class culture, they must be accepted by the local community in spite of the way in which they make their money, and (as the theory is mainly concerned with adolescence) there must be contact between the adolescent and the adult criminal world to make criminal *innovation* a step in a genuine life-long career structure.

Of course, not all those who are motivated to either destructive behaviour or innovation will find the appropriate local conditions for realizing their aspirations. Others will be prevented from engaging in either of these forms of deviance by personal scruples. For them there is no alternative but that of retreat. Cloward and Ohlin here return to Merton's concept of *retreatism* as they did with the concept of *innovation,* when they seek for an explanation of drug addiction or excessive drinking among the young.

Just as the view that deviance is due to psychological abnormality has led to a vogue for the psychological treatment of deviants, so one would expect a theory such as that of *anomie,* which sees the explanation to lie in defects in the social structure, to lead to action to eliminate those defects. Although the fear of commitment on the part of many sociologists has prevented them from going far along this reformist path, social reform implications seem to be inescapable for those who accept this theory. Hence it is different in its significance from the theory discussed earlier which postulated the coexistence of different but equally valid cultures in a society whose formal institutions are dominated by the ideas of one of those cultures. In this latter case there is no implication of either personal or social sickness; conflict and therefore deviance are seen as endemic in all societies, part of the way in which all societies operate, and therefore calling for, and susceptible to, no remedies.

But irrespective of what a society ought to do about deviance, what in fact does it do? The short answer is that it sets out to eliminate it. Just as nature is said to abhor a vacuum, so does social research suggest that societies abhor deviance. Carefully designed experiments with small groups in the laboratory have shown how powerfully the group attacks the non-conformist, attempting by all the means at its disposal to make him toe the line. Natural communities outside the laboratory are equally intolerant of the dissenter. It is not therefore surprising that the official institutions of our society include agencies and measures designed to produce conformity. These agencies include not only the penal system, which is perhaps the most striking example, but also the mental health services, the various personal social services, and so forth.

Durkheim argued that, at an earlier stage in the development of society, dominant social norms were invested with a strong moral aura, the deviant being looked upon as a wicked person. At one time even the mentally sick were punished. Although such barbaric treatment of the insane whom we now accept as unable to help themselves has largely ceased, 'blaming' is still the most important element in our attitude to criminals. Generally speaking, the criminal is assumed to be responsible for his actions, and therefore due to receive punishment in proportion to the degree of 'wickedness' of those actions. As sociological and psychological research on the causes of criminality has advanced, this moralistic approach has been combined with a more practical attitude. In other words, society is now not solely concerned with allocating blame, but also with trying to change the behaviour in question; what Durkheim called restitutive law has come more into the picture.

Originally, this took the form of deterrence. Punishment would be aimed at making it unprofitable to continue with criminal behaviour. This is still an important penal motive, but it is limited in at least two ways. In the first place it assumes that criminals always calmly and shrewdly calculate profit and loss before embarking on their crimes, whereas it is known that many crimes, and especially crimes of violence, are often committed on impulse. The second limitation on the usefulness of deterrence arises from the uncertainty of punishment after a crime has been committed. Fewer than half of the crimes known to the police are actually solved by them; in all the other cases the crime remains undetected. In addition an even larger number of crimes remains unreported and therefore unknown even to the police, representing the so-called 'dark figure' of criminality. As every schoolboy knows, the deterrent force of a threat of punishment is affected much less by the severity of the threat than by the likelihood of its being carried out. The threats of the penal system are carried into effect in such a relatively small proportion of the total cases of criminal behaviour as to leave plenty of room for even a 'calculating' criminal to argue, 'I shan't be caught'.

For reasons such as this, more subtle approaches have been adopted, especially since the war. These involve the use of psychiatric or psychological treatment, or the employment of caseworkers such as prison welfare officers or probation officers. Their aim is not to blame the criminal as in the traditional penal philosophy, nor primarily to deter him, but to help him to discover the error of his ways. This change to a persuasive approach has been accompanied by the emergence of a new conception of the nature of crime itself. Crime is often seen as a form of mental or social sickness in the individual and the work of the psychologist or the social worker is described as *treatment*. In other words, the criminal is not really responsible for his behaviour, which, it is held, is the result of some kind of disease process. Nothing indeed could be more different from the older moralistic

153

L

system. Nothing indeed could be more at odds with traditional conceptions of justice, which still aim to 'make the punishment fit the crime'. This represents a genuine dilemma for our judges, who have been brought up to administer justice but are now required very often to apply conceptions of treatment which clash with this. Somebody may, for example, receive a shorter or a longer sentence than would have been the case had justice been done in the traditional manner, because such a sentence is considered necessary for his rehabilitiation.

Much the same change has occurred in our way of dealing with other than criminal forms of deviance. Problem families or neglectful mothers would have been treated a few years ago as wicked people deserving punishment. Nowadays they are likely to be approached by social caseworkers who set out to help them to adopt a way of life more in confirmity with that of the respectable classes in society. Thus, although the work of social workers, and to some extent also that of psychologists and psychiatrists, may seem to be concerned with aiming at an objective state of social or psychological health, which all healthy people would accept as desirable, they are to a large extent engaged instead in the transmission of a set of cultural norms. To exactly the same extent as earlier and more deterrent approaches, they are endeavouring to produce social conformity. The difference is in the methods which they use. These are subtler and related more realistically to the nature of the forces which shape behaviour. None of this ought to surprise us. Like the penal system, the social services are provided by those with power in our society to serve purposes of their own. Those purposes were once legitimated by being equated with morality; now they are legitimated by being equated with health.

Whether these efforts are effective or not will depend to a very large extent upon whether the deviance they seek to eliminate is a result of mental or social sickness, or not. This, as we have seen, is one approach to the problem, although, if it is a social sickness arising from defects in the structure of society itself (*anomie,* for example), the most effective cure is likely to be found through social reform rather than reformative work with individuals. If, on the other hand, deviance is a natural state resulting from inter-group conflicts inherent in all societies, then ideas of treatment are inappropriate because there is nothing to 'cure'. In these circumstances the coercion of an unwilling minority into submission through some deterrent measure or other, though unattractive, seems more realistic.

The difficulty is to make deterrence effective. In the end the existence of a permanent group of dissidents seems to be acknowledged by the extent to which the agencies who work with them concentrate upon simply 'containing' them. Thus the reformative and deterrent aspects of our prisons are relatively unimportant as compared with containment aspects. Much the most important thing is to ensure that prisoners do not escape, or make a disturbance which is likely to reach the notice of members of the respectable community outside. For instance, a year or so ago, a few prison escapes led to setting up the Mountbatten Committee and, as a result, the halting of progress towards more rehabilitation in prisons in the interests of greater security. For offenders who are perceived as less intractable, as in the case of those placed on probation, containment measures have always been advocated less, and therapeutic measures more.

Much sociological research has been directed towards residential establishments set up to deal with deviance, such as mental hospitals and prisons. Goffman has pointed to the similarity between such residential institutions and army camps and monasteries. Calling them all *total institutions,* he shows how the individual is required, on entry, to lose his outside identity and to acquire another more standardized identity. Thus the monk, the soldier, and the prisoner are required to restrict their contacts with the outside world, to change their clothes and sometimes their property for a standard institutional issue, to replace their names by a number or a religious name, and then by a series of often humiliating initiatory rituals to accept their new station in life, the much humbler one of being a cog in the machine.

The total institution is total in the sense that virtually all of the individual's life activities go on within it. Whereas you and I may work, eat, sleep and play in different places with different groups of people, the inmate of the total institution has to satisfy all these needs within the walls of the institution. With a body of inmates who are processed to its specifications, this kind of institution has obviously a very high capacity to preserve itself and to serve a social function, such as the containment function of the prison.

All of this assumes that human beings are more malleable than they really are, that their hereditary qualities, as well as those which they have acquired through their experience to date, are as nothing when compared with the forces of indoctrination brought to bear upon them by the total institution. The research of Sykes and Schrag suggest that this is far from being the case.[8] While the inmates of a prison may pay lip-service to the demands of the institution they build up their own relationships with one another under the surface, and thus establish a kind of underground society, which is not only more satisfying to the kind of people they really are, but by setting itself up in opposition to the institutional régime, actually tries to compensate the inmates for the deprivations imposed upon them by that régime.

Every experienced prison administrator knows that, in addition to the superficial world of conformity and obedience there is in every prison an inmate culture of this kind which is often very criminal and very hostile to authority. It attempts in Sykes' phrase to 'lessen the pain of imprisonment' by the unwritten laws which inmates enforce among themselves. They are expected to support each other against the staff and to help each other to secure as many pleasures and privileges as possible while in prison. 'Playing it cool' and standing up to authority are other maxims. Tobacco becomes the inmate 'money', with which they can buy most things, from a suit which fits better than the official issue, to occasional delicacies stolen from the prison kitchen.

It would be a mistake to idealize this community of criminals. Although the unwritten law calls for inmate solidarity and mutual aid, this loyalty is in conflict with previous experience, for criminal behaviour emphasizes quite different standards as well, such as exploitation or betrayal, if they pay. Although the old saying that there is no honour among thieves does go too far, it would be equally foolish to take the maxims of the inmate code of the prison at their face value. There is therefore much violence, much dishonesty, and considerable exploitation in the prison underworld. The most striking example of this is the institution of the 'baron'. The tobacco baron is a kind of banker, who lends tobacco to people who cannot afford to buy it. They may then of course use it either as money, to buy something else, or to smoke. Generally it is in demand for smoking, and as the baron extorts a very high rate of interest, it is not long before a substantial part of the inmate community is in debt to him. He employs a group of prisoners in his business, either as custodians of his stock of tobacco (which he disperses in this way as a safeguard against discovery by the authorities), as tobacco distributors, or as 'strong arm men' to coerce those who do not pay their debts. The baron is a powerful and corrupting figure in all English prisons. In some large local prisons he probably has more real power than the governor himself.

It is easy to see the difficulties which confront attempts at rehabilitation within the prison. The prisoner spends most of his time not with the rehabilitative staff, but with other criminals, and in a climate which is hostile to the staff and their objectives. If he conforms it will be in order to be left alone by the staff. This is the aim of most prisoners, doing time the easy way or, in their own vernacular, 'doing bird'. But if this situation is not conducive to rehabilitation it is perfectly consistent with the containment motive, which ensures superficially good behaviour on the part of the prisoners, so long as they are indeed left alone.

The question is now being raised as to whether, from the point of view of eliminating deviance, there is much point in sending people away from home. If the problem does arise mainly out of the social relationships of the deviant, to send him away is merely to put it into abeyance. Any effective action must be directed to the relationships themselves, i.e., it must be carried through while he is still living within his own outside community, with all those relationships intact and active in producing deviance. For such reasons there is a trend at present against residential institutions not only for offenders, but also for deprived children and the aged. The current preference for the community care of the mentally ill who would previously have been treated in mental hospitals is along the same lines.

The social ecologists had seen their task in just such a context. Believing that the heart of the problem was the tradition of deviance in blighted areas, they felt it was this which had to be tackled, and that no purpose was served by trying to change individuals in isolation. Thus emerged the Chicago Area Projects, pioneer experiments with a new social work technique called community organization, in which the task of the social worker was to stimulate the local community into recognizing and tackling its own social problems. All of which assumes that the members of such a community come to see their behaviour as a problem. As was said earlier, everything depends on who is to say what the problem is. Those with power and influence in society are able to influence how the law and the social services define a problem. Those groups whose behaviour is stigmatized as problem behaviour may have a different view of the matter. It may take more than skilled social work to convince them that they are wrong when they define as problem behaviour, not their own actions, but those of the more powerful groups who harrass them.

SUGGESTED READING

WILLS, W. DAVID, *The Barns Experiment* (Allen & Unwin, 1947).
JONES, HOWARD, *Crime in a Changing Society* (Penguin Books, 1965).
SYKES, G. M., *The Society of Captives* (Princeton University Press, 1968).
AICHORN, A., *Wayward Youth* (Viking Press, 1965).
COHEN, A. K., *Deviance and Control* (New Jersey: Prentice-Hall, 1966).
BOWLBY, J., *et al.*, *Maternal Deprivation* (Geneva: W.H.O.).
GOFFMAN, E., *Asylums* (New York: Doubleday, 1965).
WOLFGANG, M., *et al.*, *Sociology of Crime and Delinquency* (New York: Wiley, 1962).
JOHNSTON, N., *et al.*, *Sociology of Punishment and Correction* (New York: Wiley, 1962).

NOTES

1 *Maternal Care and Mental Health* (Geneva: W.H.O., 1952).
2 *Crime and Personality* (Routledge & Kegan Paul, 1964).
3 *Principles of Criminology* (with D. R. Cressey) (Philadelphia: Lippincott, sixth edition, 1960).
4 *Delinquency and Drift* (New York: Wiley, 1964).
5 *Other People's Money* (Glencoe, Illinois: Free Press, 1953).
6 *Suicides and Homicide* (Glencoe, Illinois: Free Press, 1954).
7 *Delinquency and Opportunity* (Routledge & Kegan Paul, 1961).
8 G. M. Sykes, *Society of Captives* (Princeton University Press, 1958); C. Schrag, 'Some Foundations for a Theory of Corrections, in *The Prison*, edited by D. R. Cressey (Holt, Rinehart & Winston, 1961).

7

Applied Sociology

Albert B. Cherns

There is a traditional expectation that when we pick up a book on science we shall see first the subject-matter of the science set out, its discoveries 'and its methods and that at the end of the book we shall find a chapter on *applications*—the hardware end of the business. At this point we expect that we shall now see examples of ingenuity, but that we shall not learn about advances in the science itself. In fact, in many sciences the technology has been in the lead and scientific explanation has been obliged to catch up with its applications. In the social sciences the relationship is even less clear-cut. For one thing, it is not the simplest thing in the world to explain what we mean by *applied sociology*. We understand what is meant by applied mathematics, applied physics and so on, but when we come to the social sciences the distinction between what is done in the laboratory and what is done by practitioners is less clear. After all, the world of human behaviour is the social scientist's laboratory, and it is seldom that we can get very far by thinking about social phenomena in the abstract.

There is a model which we tend to carry around in our heads of the relationship between research, development and application which is derived from a misunderstanding of these processes in the physical sciences. We think of pure research being done in back rooms, resulting in a scientific breakthrough which is then picked up and developed in industrial laboratories, finally to be put into application in the form of production. People who have studied this in detail have found that such a linear process can seldom be observed. The process is a much more untidy one than this simple model proposes. In the social sciences the process is often closer to the medical model, where advances in practice feed back into the laboratory :

> In the natural sciences, the fundamental data are reached by abstracting the phenomena to be studied from their natural contexts and submitting them to basic research through experimental manipulation in a laboratory. It is only then that a second process of applied research is set under way. The social scientist can use these methods only to a limited extent ... the social scientist begins in practice, however imperfect scientifically, and works back to theory and the more systematic research which may test this, and then back again to improved practice. Though this way of working is well understood in the case of medicine, it is not so well understood, even among social scientists, that the same type of model applies to a very wide range of social science activities.[1]

Thus, applied sociology is not just the application of sociological research findings to practical situations, and applied sociology can mean many things. The term is often used as synonymous with empirical sociology, which again is used to mean sociological research in which field data is collected. This brings so much of sociology into its province that it is not a very helpful usage. A more useful distinction is between theory-oriented and field- or problem-oriented research. Very similar empirical studies might be mounted in one case to throw light on a theoretical problem and in another case to solve a practical problem. Often, as we shall show, research undertaken with the latter motive may add significantly to the development of sociological concepts, while theory-oriented research may also develop notions or uncover facts which may throw light on a social problem.

The methods of applied sociology then are essentially the methods of sociology and a piece of work may be described as 'applied' sociology when the concepts, categories and techniques of research and study in sociology are applied to some real world problem. Looked at in this light, a good deal of present-day market research can be regarded as applied sociology, although in many cases the practitioners are not themselves sociologists. We shall not be discussing this kind of application, but rather the application of research to new problems; in other words, once a line has been developed, once the techniques and methods have been made a matter of routine, and once we can hand over the practice to a layman, we can cease to think of it as applied sociological research.

The applied sociologist may need to use other methods besides those of sociology itself. The sociologist, for example, who seeks to estimate the effectiveness of some social welfare policy, or of some industrial organization, may need to use the methods of the operational researcher; that is to say, he will need to establish what are the objectives of the organization he is studying, what criteria he can develop to measure or assess the extent to which these goals are achieved, as well as the relationship of these criteria to the sociological data he is using. More recently still we shall find sociologists using methods of action research with which they positively intervene in the organization that they are studying so as to study the impact of changes that they have proposed.

Applied sociology is in this sense concerned with the interaction of the principles and methods of sociology with real situations leading to the development and modification of sociological ideas and methods. Robert C. Angell has offered a most useful definition of applied sociology: 'When sociology is not an end in itself, but becomes a means to some other end, it is applied sociology.' We should suggest the slight modification : 'When sociology is not *the only* end in itself, but becomes, at least partly, a means to some other end, it is applied sociology.'

We shall have something to say at the end of this chapter about the problems of application and utilization of sociological research. This is by no means a straightforward matter. To begin with, problems as they appear to be seen by policy-makers, managers, administrators, do not clothe themselves in sociological categories, and for the sociologist to contribute towards their solution, or even their illumination, he needs to re-frame them in other terms. Thus, for example, in Israel a housing development agency asked sociologists how they would design a neighbourhood so as to make possible the integration of people from different ethnic backgrounds. They had in mind the question of how you could lay out buildings into a pattern to achieve this kind of integration. Whether this is possible or not, it is not a sociological question. The sociologist had to reinterpret the question into one of how you allocate families of different backgrounds to houses in such a way as to maximize the possibilities of integration. Because the differences in approach between administrators and sociologists were not made explicit, the sponsors were disappointed in the report and the recommendations they received. But this is another story.

Even if the administrator and the sociologist can agree on how to frame the problem, the sociologist's analysis may not be acceptable: for one thing, the administrator may deny the rationality of the analysis; but, even when he is prepared to accept it, he may point out that the solution would be impracticable for political or administrative reasons which lay outside the sociologist's frame of reference. For him, administration is the art of the possible and what is possible may not include solutions which involve changing the relative power of different people or groups. People in organizations have a way of seeing conflict in personal terms and they find it very hard to see that workers may have different goals from those of the organization. Production engineers see inspectors and quality-control experts as awkward people and are seen in their turn as obstinate and out only for quantity. To the sociologist it may be clear that these are not personality traits, but aspects of the roles that their job responsibilities require. We may see the same pattern in the mutual views of policy-maker and sociologist, and part of the process of applying sociology is indeed their mutual learning. In order to apply the insights of the sociologists, the policy-makers and administrators have to learn a little sociology and acquire not only the vocabulary, but the insights to be derived from the proper use of such terms as *role, reference group, primary social relations* and *stratification* and so on. Thus to some extent the applied sociologist has to teach his 'clients' some of the rudiments of his science. All this helps to explain why it is difficult to pick up the results of sociological research and use them to solve problems. It is a sophisticated process and requires a degree of analysis of the problem in its setting, which cannot be left to non-sociologists. Thus, this chapter will not contain a set of recipes, but descriptions from a number of selected studies. The aim is to show the sorts of insights into practical problems in society that are provided by sociological analysis.

Urban Sociology

In a sense urban sociology is the whole discipline of sociology; after all, the main distinction between the anthropologist and the sociologist is that the former studies small-scale tribal societies, while the latter studies modern large-scale societies; and modern large-scale societies are predominantly urban in character. So, when we talk about urban sociology we are trying to make a distinction between those aspects of modern society which derive especially from urban development and those that do not. Urban society was studied extensively in many aspects by the Chicago School of Sociologists in the 1930s and culminated in Louis Wirth's article 'Urbanism as a Way of Life'. In this he contrasted the kinds of relationship of traditional rural society with those of the dweller in the city for, as he put it, the city dweller's social contacts become 'impersonal, superficial, transistory and segmental'. The city dweller tends to treat social relationships as a means to his own ends. Greater differentiation and specialization are required: people spend different parts of their day in different activities in different areas of the city. The close web of social relationships, typical of the rural community, is replaced by the more impersonal style of relationship of urban society. Into this analysis gets mixed a kind of romanticism which views the rural past as a golden age of self-reliant but mutually supportive individuals in large extended families, all of whose activities are integrated into the community. This is seen as superseded by a hurrying, scurrying, impersonal ant-heap in which each member is busy about his own affairs, returning to his 'nuclear' family of wife and children, in some impersonal suburb.

Certainly the development of the city has brought profound changes in people's lives, although, of course, the city is not a new invention. Nor are problems of multi-racial societies new either, although the modern city shows some of them in their most acute form. The modern city, typically, is multi-racial, pluralistic (by which we mean that there are many different sources of power, influence and status in the society), and require for their day-to-day survival complex essential services. Living in such a city requires the development of new roles for social institutions of all kinds, including government and local government, churches, schools; and, in particular, it has brought changes in the role, stability and function of the family. With their specific interest in the family as an institution, sociologists have naturally given considerable study to these changes. Sometimes the motive for the study has been a welfare one, directly inspired by the need to do something about a social problem : poverty, slum housing, delinquency, and so on; sometimes the study has been motivated by sociological goals, that is, to test out beliefs, hypotheses and assertions about the impact of urban living on family life. Here we see the complex interaction of pure empirical and applied sociology, because some of the applied studies have resulted in developments of theory and some of the pure empirical studies have helped to guide social action.

As an example of the first, we may take the study of Elizabeth Bott entitled *Family and Social Network,* 1957. This started from the need to develop casework methods for the family welfare associations and was indeed successful in doing so. In the course of her studies she found, as others had found, that there was a great deal of variation in the

165

extent to which husbands and wives carried out their activities separately and independently of each other. To this
Elizabeth Bott added the discovery that the degree of *conjugal segregation* (the extent to which the roles of husband
and wife were different and distinct) was related to the
pattern of relationship maintained by members of the family
with external people, and the relationships of these external
people with one another. As she put it:

> The immediate social environment of an urban family
> consists of a network rather than an organized group ...
> In all societies elementary families have a network of social
> relationships. But in many small-scale societies with a
> simple division of labour, elementary families are also con-
> cerned with organized groups that control many aspects of
> their daily activities. Urban families are not completely
> encapsulated by organized groups in this way ... The
> networks of urban families vary in degree of connected-
> ness, namely in the extent to which the people with whom
> the family maintains relationships carry on relationships
> with one another. These variations in network-connected-
> ness are particularly evident in informal relationships be-
> tween friends, neighbours and relatives. Such differences
> in connectedness are associated with differences in degree
> of segregation of conjugal roles. The degree of segregation
> in the role-relationship of husband and wife varies directly
> with the connectedness of the family's social network ...
> If husband and wife come to marriage with closeknit
> networks, and if conditions are such that this pattern of
> relationships can be continued, the marriage is superim-
> posed on the previous relationships and each partner con-
> tinues to be drawn into activities with outside people ...
> Rigid segregation of conjugal roles is possible because each
> partner can get help from people outside. But if husband
> and wife come to marriage with loose-knit networks, or if
> their networks become loose-knit after marriage, they must
> seek in each other some of the emotional satisfaction and
> help with familial tasks that couples in close-knit networks
> can get from outsiders. Joint organization becomes more

necessary for the success of the family as an enterprise . . .
Many clinical workers, doctors, and family research
workers take it for granted that joint organization is the
natural and normal form for familial behaviour to take.
Advice based on this assumption must be rather bewilder-
ing to families in close-knit networks (pp. 216–18).

These observations have been a contribution to our understanding of the role of the family in modern urban society,
as well as helping towards the development of casework
method.

Let us compare this with *Family and Kinship in East
London,* 1957, by M. Young and P. Willmott, who doubted
the truth of the assumptions made about the impersonal
urban culture. In their research they studied families in
Bethnal Green (a traditional working-class suburb) and they
found many of the characteristics of village society persisted:
people knew their neighbours and a good deal about their
neighbours' business; they saw other members of the family
frequently, even daily; and, typically, the wife's mother
lived nearby and saw her daughter every day. Although the
environment was dismal, even seedy, from the point of view
of the outsider, it provided warmth and personal contact
and neighbourliness for its inhabitants. Again, although
households may typically consist of nuclear families, the
closeness of grandparents, aunts and even cousins means
that children grow up within an extended family.

Young and Willmott then went on to a study of families
moved to a new housing estate which they called 'Greenleigh'.
This was a clean, new suburb and to the outsider appeared
a much more favourable environment than Bethnal Green.
To many of the families moved there, however, the change
was seen as a bad one: it was no longer possible for daughter
to see mother every day and the close companionship and
social networks were broken. This study was only one of
several which developed these themes and it is quoted here
because in many ways it was the most influential in its
popular interpretation; it tended to develop into a picture

of a monstrous working class 'Mum', cleaving her family to her and dominating them without mercy.

Other studies have demonstrated the wide variety of urban communities that exist in Britain and while Madeline Kerr's study *The People of Ship Street*, 1958, showed a matriarchal society similar to that of Bethnal Green, the authors of *Coal is our Life*, 1956, depicted a strongly patriarchal system in the coalfield. This again appears to be more typical of older towns focused on traditional industries. Where son followed father into the pit or the works and formed a member of a team of mates in which seniority granted status, the family developed among its functions that of protecting and serving the breadwinner, and the son soon learned to adopt the dominant masculine role.

These studies have proved very influential among social workers and have done much to alert planners to the defects of a good deal of post-war development of housing estates and new towns. Other studies have concentrated more on specific social problems, although in nearly every case they have pinpointed the importance of the family in modern, as in traditional society. Studies of old people have mostly had welfare motivations for their origin. We see that modern medicine and hygiene have helped to keep alive a larger proportion of people beyond the age of retirement. This, together with the trend towards smaller families, means that old people are a much higher proportion of the total of the population than at any time in the past. Assumptions about the breakdown of the old extended family conduced towards the picture of lonely and deserted old people, many living on the margins of poverty. The reality is often sadly close to the picture, but it turns out that families do much more for their elderly members than is popularly believed. Furthermore, international comparisons appear to show the falsity of the idea that the development of the welfare state reduced the role of the family in looking after the old. Countries with even more centralized welfare provision than Britain and countries with less, differ little from Britain in the proportion of the elderly receiving aid and shelter from their families.

At the other end of the age scale there have been many studies of children in need of care, in particular, delinquent children, and there have been studies of the effects on their family, especially the children, of married women taking employment. There have been studies also of disorganized families and the effect on their individual members. In the process of urbanization, clearly the family has undergone changes in the demands put upon it from outside and the needs of its members for which it has to cater. It would appear to be a very robust institution and one whose role even now needs more study. After all, the family is the main organ of socialization of the individual and thus appears to be able to produce at different times and in different situations individuals who will fit into all kinds of societies—totalitarian, democratic, capitalist, socialist, etc. The way in which it carries out these functions brings us into the realm of social psychology and social anthropology, but from the work of the urban sociologist a good deal of evidence has accumulated about the relevance of child-rearing practices to the personality and style of the typical member of the community. This evidence has been brought together by Josephine Klein in her two-volumed work, *Samples from English Cultures*, 1965.

We end where we began: Britain, in particular, has a long tradition of anti-urbanism. We look on the true old England as the countryside and village life, although Britain is one of the most urban countries in the world and was the first to become predominantly urban. Until very recently practically all children's story-books were about Jack and Jill in the village, with the village postman, the village policeman, the village parson, and the village schoolteacher, not to mention the village squire, as focal characters, and we are brought up to think that urbanization is somehow contaminating. Only now are we beginning to see how successfully on the whole the constitution of the family has adapted itself, how life persists within the city and how important is the compensating variety of experience which the town traditionally offers and the village does not.

169

Sociology of Industry

With the growing success of mechanical contrivances and the increase in number and scale of factories, the task and skills of the production worker have undergone dramatic change. Early in this century the typical worker in the most advanced sectors of industry would be a machine operator. As the old craft skills declined and semi-skilled machine operations took their place, the variability and inefficiency of the man compared with the machine became apparent. Led by the famous F. W. Taylor, the Scientific Management School emerged: their doctrine was that of the 'one best way'. Scientific analysis of every job would lead to the design of the most efficient set of movements for achieving it. These movements would be economical in number and in the use of muscle groups. With training and adequate incentives a worker would then produce twice or three times what he did before, or even more. Many managements adopted the tenets of scientific management and its associated technique of time-and-motion study. Of course this did not always work and, when it did, workers were producing less than they might, and this was seen as restriction of output, for which no satisfactory reason could be adduced.

The famous Hawthorne experiments of the late 'twenties and early 'thirties in America appeared to show, among other things, that these restrictions on output were imposed by the informal groups to which workers belonged. It is difficult to summarize very briefly the Hawthorne experiments: they were designed to discover by patient experiment the optimum blend of environmental conditions, hours of work, number and duration of rest pauses, welfare and canteen provisions and so on. The experimenters systematically altered one variable at a time while trying to maintain all others unchanged. In order the better to observe them, the experimenters hived off into one room a number of female operators, and many of the measurements were made on their performance. With each successive change in working conditions the girls' output went up until the experimenters' suspicions were aroused. They then removed all the changes, restoring the position to what it had been before the experiments began. Output continued to rise. Among the explanations that the experimenters offered were the following: the style of supervision in the small room was more permissive and friendly than before; the girls were responding to the fact of being observed, to having notice taken and interest shown in them. They appeared to develop a strong group feeling and the group was oriented towards increasing productivity, partly to please the supervisors and partly to please the experimenters, and partly to satisfy the financial needs of their most hard-pressed colleagues. From these, and other findings, developed the human relations movement, which broadly worked on the belief that, alongside the formal organization of an enterprise, an informal organization develops with its own goals and norms; the goals of the informal organization must be aligned with those of the formal organizations and the method was that of a permissive form of leadership which allowed the worker to identify with the supervisor. Training courses for managers and supervisors were developed and without a doubt many industrial enterprises became pleasanter places in which to work. But it soon appeared that the expected relationship between morale and productivity did not result. Under some circumstances it did; under others it did not.

At this point it is fair to say the sociologist first enters the picture. Until then contributions had been made by the engineer, the physiologist, the psychologist and finally the social psychologist. The sociologist had been more interested in the major themes of industrialization and class conflict. With the sociologist came the notion of structure and of structural conflict. The Human Relations School assumed that the basic aims of the worker and management should not be in conflict: for both, the good of the enterprise meant more security and more pay; but this does not represent the way the worker has learned to see industrial history. Greater profits have not always resulted in better security for the worker; more output per worker may mean fewer workers. It is not unreasonable then for working groups under certain circumstances to pursue aims which differ markedly from those of their employers.

Tom Lupton showed that workers' restrictive practices were often far more rational than had been thought.[2] He studied factories in two different industries in Manchester : one a garment factory, the other a heavy electrical engineering concern. In the first there was little sign of the systematic restriction of output that characterized the second. Where management control of the supply of work was inadequate either due to the quality of the management or to inefficiences in the supply of parts or to the inherent difficulties in the trade, the workers developed a method of 'fiddling' which served to maintain their weekly earnings at a predictable level. They were, in fact, effectively protecting themselves against the uncertainties to which they were subjected. The structure of an industry, its market situation, its traditional practices and the way work is organized to fit in with the characteristics of the manufacturing processes and raw materials, all influence the practices workers adopt.

The effect that different kinds of technology have on management and on industrial relations was the subject of Joan Woodward's famous study, *Industrial Organization: Theories and Practice,* 1964. Management theorists, rather like Taylor, had developed a universal model for management organization. Joan Woodward wanted to see whether firms which adhered to the model were more successful than those which did not. The theorists laid down principles concerning the number of people who should report to one boss, the number of levels of organization that there should be, the way in which functions should be assigned, and so on. Joan Woodward found the extent to which firms were successful bore no relationship to their practice in any of these respects; nor did it appear that such factors as size of firm, type of ownership and so on were associated with these factors either. She then grouped firms into categories according to their technology, and in its simplest form her method reduced firms to three categories : unit and small-batch production; large-batch and mass production; and process production. Now she found that firms in each of these groups tended towards a similar pattern of organization. There were much larger differences *between* the groups than *within* them. Furthermore it appeared that the most successful firms in each group were those whose practices were closest to the norms of their group. Yet another finding was that the group which came closest to adhering to the prescriptions of the management theorists were those in large-batch and mass production. As she points out, the heyday of the management theorists came in the 1930s in the United States when the most advanced type of manufacturing technology was mass production, with the motor-car assembly plant as its exemplar. In the typical mass-production assembly line the group of workers in the most crucial function (production) are semi-skilled machine-minders. The tone of management/worker relations in such a plant takes its flavour from management control of semi-skilled production workers. This tone is quite different from that in unit and small-batch production where the typical production workers are skilled craftsmen, and from that in process production where the most important function for workers is not concerned with production at all, but with process control and maintenance and which require comparatively high skill. Thus the tone of industrial relations in both unit and process production is pleasanter, more comradely and less conflict-ridden than in mass production.

The importance of the form which communication takes within the enterprise has been emphasized by the work of Tom Burns.[3] With George Stalker, he studied electronics firms in Scotland, adapting after the war to a change in their market situation from a single government defence market to a highly competitive commercial one. In these circumstances there was a premium on the ability of management to manage innovation, and the crucial issue was its ability to obtain results from its research and development division. They found two polar-types of organization: the organic and the mechanistic. The latter corresponded closely to the 'ideal bureaucratic' pattern: jobs and responsibility were clearly defined, communications flowed down and up the management hierarchy as pictured on the organization chart,

173

people knew the extent of their responsibilities and could draw a line beyond which what happened was 'no business of theirs'. By contrast, the organic type was far more chaotic in appearance: typically there was more communication across the chart than up and down it (i.e., managers communicated more with their colleagues in other functional divisions of the organization than with their own boss); people from different divisions formed project-type groups; the boundaries of responsibilities were not sharply drawn and might change from time to time, even day to day. The managing director could not pick up the telephone and be sure that Mr X would be in his office. Burns and Stalker found that the latter type of firm was far more successful in adapting to innovation than the former. They did not conclude, however, that organic type firms were necessarily better than mechanistic types at all times; indeed, in static conditions the mechanistic type of operation may have considerable advantages. For one thing, it is far less wearing on the nerves. Firms, in fact, tend to behave in a more or less mechanistic way at different times, but it does appear that those which cannot function in an organic way have not the flexibility to respond to the demands of technological advance or of market development.

What both Woodward's and Burns's studies have shown is that there is no single best form of organization. Given its primary task; an enterprise is faced with a choice both of technologies and of organization. There has to be a fit between the two. The Tavistock Institute of Human Relations developed this notion into their concept of a *sociotechnical system*. Essentially, what is meant by this is that any technical system has to be operated by people and these people have to be organized. The organized group of people form a social system, interacting with the technical one at every point where men operate, maintain or monitor machines (i.e. at every 'man-machine interface'). Any change of the technical system will produce changes affecting the social system, either because people have to change their tasks or the way in which they perform tasks, or their interrelationships with one another change. The social system in turn will adapt to these changes in a way which is determined partly by the dynamics of social systems and partly by the relationships that this particular system has with others outside. Frequently, the way in which the social system responds tends to frustrate the effects intended by the devisers of the technical change. The most dramatic example reported by the Tavistock Institute was the effect of the introduction of modern machinery in coal-mining.[4] Under the previous system groups of miners undertook the entire cycle of processes in the pits : coal-cutting; removing; the preparation for further advance, involving the installation of pit-props and so on. With the advent of the new machinery each phase of the cycle was allocated to one shift. It turned out that the new technology produced far less output than had been anticipated and forecast. The roots of the trouble turned out to lie in a misfit between the social and technical systems. Miners in different shifts no longer felt that they could rely on those who were responsible for other phases of the cycle to do their jobs in a way that made their own profitable and safe. The group cohesion of the old system had been lost. Absenteeism, sickness and accident rates were higher. Groups of miners got together to work out a system which gave more satisfaction to their needs. A form of organization emerged which re-introduced some of the aspects of the old system; morale improved and with it output. The organizational choice apparently favoured by the men and clearly favoured by the Institute is one which leads to what the Institute describes as 'non-alienated work roles', and they point out how much our forms of industrial organization have rested on the assumption the worker will be 'alienated' from his work and bribed by his financial return to endure it.

J. H. Goldthorpe and others in *The Affluent Worker*, 1968, have demonstrated how this type of role fits the trend towards family- and house-centred living. The so-called 'affluent worker' may choose to do a well-paid manual job even though it may involve a lower skill than he is capable of. His rewards are ownership of a house, a car and a seaside holiday for his family. Much of his spare time is devoted to his house and garden and his leisure is spent more with his family than with this workmates.[5] This picture is in stark contrast to that of the traditional working class in the older, more traditional industries, such as mining and steel. We see here the influence of environmental factors on what happens inside the plant, the mill or the pit.

Thus the original concept of a sociotechnical system has had to be widened to that of an open system, in dynamic equilibrium with its environment. Some roles occupy the boundary between the enterprise and its environment and have to manage transaction across these boundaries, for example, dealing with customers or the public. Workers in the Institute for Social Research at Michigan have shown that these boundary roles are the ones which involve greatest stress for their occupants. Less attention has been given to the boundaries which exist within an enterprise and when they are studied they are found to be often poorly defined. Trouble comes when the boundaries between departments do not correspond to the natural breaks in the processes of production or distribution. Much of the observable inefficiency and confusion in industrial organizations is traceable to attempts to control boundaries which are in the wrong place, or to regulate processes whose discontinuities have not been matched by adequate organizational devices.

In this section, we have picked out only a few of the themes in industrial sociology and given particular attention to those developed in Britain. A section on industrial sociology written from an American viewpoint or from a French viewpoint would look different and the full story would take not a section in a chapter, but a large book.

The Sociology of Custodial Institutions and Mental Health

One of the most interesting fields of work for the sociologist has been in the way in which society deals with its temporary or permanent failures. Any society has to be protected against those who persistently flout its values, but it also has to take steps to contain those whose adjustment to its demands is so inadequate that they are a source of danger to themselves

176

or to others. Thus a class of institutions grows up which seldom has much claim on the resources of society and about which people prefer to know very little. This attitude of society has been described as one of *isolation and denial,* and it covers the public attitude towards prisons, mental hospitals and mental illness itself. This whole area of study has a good deal in common both with the study of other social institutions and with that of mental health generally. Thus, we shall find ourselves discussing these problems in two contexts : that of total institutions and that of mental health. Total institutions is a term which has been used by Erving Goffman in his book, *Asylums,* 1961, to describe institutions of which membership is not voluntary, or at any rate in which termination of membership is not by voluntary action, and in which the individuals are 'inmates', that is to say, their whole life is controlled by the institutions and their contacts with the world outside are not direct, but are mediated by the institutions. Clearly, prisons are total institutions in this sense; mental hospitals only slightly less so; boarding schools are to some extent, and ships at sea and military units are, in varying degrees, total institutions. They turn out to be characterized by an institutional culture, and one strange characteristic of this culture is that even where membership is involuntary and where the inmates may be struggling to get out, the maintenance of the system depends on their co-operation and acceptance of the roles which are defined for them.[6] This phenomenon is achieved by a process described as *institutionalization,* whereby the individual's links with the outside world are systematically cut and he is resocialized into the culture of the institution. As Professor Jones described in Chapter 6, the first step in the process is to remove the individual's previous identity. His skills and connections in the world outside become irrelevant. He must find a new identity or accept an identity provided for him. This function is discharged in military units by the issuing of uniforms and the systematic indoctrination and initiation process, symbolically enacted on the barrack square. In the English public school initiation ceremonies of the type recorded in *Tom Brown's Schooldays* and fagging rites

177

served much the same function. Modern research has focused both on the process whereby the inmate adopts his role and on the difficulties and dilemmas of the staff, leading to the demands which they make on the inmates. To take the latter point first, society demands that the staff of penal institutions and mental hospitals should connive in the public's desire to forget that the institutions are there. They should keep the inmates out of the public's eye. They are required to serve, at the same time, three functions: the custodial, the punitive and the rehabilitative. They must keep the public secure; they must mete out punishment on behalf of the community; but they are also required to reform criminals and rehabilitate, re-educate or 'cure' the mentally disturbed. For the mental health hospital the demands of security (custodial) and of rehabilitation conflict; in the prison the demands of punishment and reform are often incompatible. Organizations which serve more than one goal tend to distribute different goals among different groups of staff. Thus the conflicts between goals become conflicts between groups of individuals. This is the situation in industrial organizations and to a large extent in mental hospitals, where the nurses tend to see the psychiatrists as dangers to the security of the hospital, while the psychiatrists are apt to see the nurses as hostile towards the goals of rehabilitation. In the prison the division is not so sharp, the goals of reform and rehabilitiation being represented more by auxiliary and visiting staff.

The existence of an institutional culture becomes apparent when one sees two wards in a hospital or two prisons or two army units, which apparently exist to serve the same function, but which differ in 'atmosphere'. In one chronic ward for the elderly you may find old people sitting around in chairs, staring into space, exchanging little communication, seemingly waiting to die. In another you may find the old people helping the attendants to make the ward look homely and cheerful.

Or we may take a comparison over time. Go back a hundred years and you will find 'lunatics' in chains, in filthy rags and in dark cells, displaying weird and violent behaviour. Now it is no longer thought necessary to restrain a psychotic, and outbreaks of violence are very rare. Of course, we have at our disposal today sedating drugs to calm the violent or to postpone and reduce attacks. But the main cause of the change is in a different set of beliefs and attitudes towards the mentally ill. Lunatics were violent very largely because they *were* restrained—if you pinion a child's arms, it will struggle violently and furiously. Restraint is a form of violence which begets frustration and rage. The appropriate role for the lunatic was raving, frothing at the mouth, and this role was quickly learnt. Similarly, the prison inmate learns his roles—to defer to the senior prisoners (the famous 'tobacco barons'), to acquire the prison jargon or argot, to adopt the right degree of subservience to the warders, while not appearing to be on such terms with them as to suggest that he is betraying the confidence of the other prisoners. What in fact the prisoner learns is a set of behaviours appropriate to the role of prisoner, a set of behaviours which validate the attitudes and behaviour of the warders. It is clear that this does not have much to do with reform of the prisoner, just as restraint had little to do with curing the insane.

We can now follow some of the changes that have taken place in the culture of mental institutions. With the help of drugs, electrical treatment and psychotherapy, it has become possible to return a large proportion of the mentally sick to their families and to the community, if not permanently, at least for long stretches of time. The emphasis has, therefore, moved towards the problems of re-integration of the patient into his family and the community. This has proceeded in several steps, starting from studies of small groups made during the war. In the process of working out new methods of officer selection, psychologists developed theories about the influence of the primary group (the face-to-face group) on its individual members. After the war the possibilities of such groups in a therapeutic role were explored, mainly by workers in the Tavistock Clinic. From this emerged the group therapy which is now a familiar feature of most mental hospitals. However, this tends to lead towards conflict be-

tween those members of the hospital staff who are involved
in the group therapy session and those who are not, and
even more between those whose roles in patient treatment
are virtually confined to the group therapy sessions and
those who are dealing with the patients for the rest of their
institutional day. This makes it difficult for the concentration
of treatment on to group therapy. In his book, *Community
as Doctor,* 1960, Robert Rapoport describes the experimental
development of a therapeutic community which used what
he called *milieu* therapy. He shows how the social Rehabilitation Unit at Belmont Hospital developed a *treatment ideology* and the problems that this set for the members of the
Unit and their relations with the rest of the hospital. He
also shows how, despite their best intentions, the members of
the unit found that while they created a community to which
patients were able to adjust and within which they could
play normal healthy roles, this did not necessarily mean
that they were fully and adequately prepared for return to
the world outside. As he points out, the unit had values
which differed considerably from those of people outside:
patients who adopted the values of the unit were successful
in the unit, but not necessarily successful outside.

The next step is towards the involvement of the outside
community in therapy and this is now being explored in
some centres in the United States. The study I have just discussed is a very good example of action research; ideas were
developed by research and tried out in the therapeutic situation. As a result of these experiments, further hypotheses
were formed and these were tried out, their results recorded
and so on, all in the context of an on-going institution. But
the experience and the results have not spread rapidly to
other psychiatric hospitals. This does not, of course, mean
that they have been lost or wasted. What has happened
follows a very familiar pattern: first, enthusiasm is gener-
ated; secondly, there is a reaction, both against the new
methods themselves and against the increased demands they
represent; thirdly, some of the results of the experience pass
into the general stock of knowledge of people working in
the field. After a number of years many of the insights have

been absorbed and used in one way or another, mostly without recognition of their source.

In our section on Industry, we show how task and organization are related, and many of the difficulties in mental hospitals arise from the fact that, since a technology for treating psychotic patients does not exist, a rational division of labour and authority cannot exist either. This is true to some extent for the military unit in a peacetime role, and further studies should throw light on these problems.

Another interesting set of studies of mental hospitals has been made by L. P. Ullmann[7] who has compared a number of such hospitals in the United States on the basis of a number of criteria. He found, for example, that there is a relationship between the size of hospitals and their effectiveness, which bears out R. W. Revans' discovery that the bigger a unit becomes the lower its morale drops. Ullmann shows how some administrative devices, not confined to hospitals, have a distorting effect on an organization: for example, in many institutions the head of a department obtains status from the size of his staff and his budget. When the time comes to allocate the budget for the coming year an increased allocation is seen as a mark of approval. This clearly does not conduce to economical practices. Further, it turns out that a hospital which discharges patients quickly, thereby, one would think, demonstrating efficiency, becomes penalized for having empty beds. Thus, increasing the number of treatment staff per patient turns out to be effective in reducing the number of patients who remain for a long time in the hospital, but is not effective in producing a higher rate of early discharges.

We may contrast the action research of Rapoport with this study, which is an example of the use of operational research methods in the social sciences. The steps are as follows: (i) the aims of the institution are elicited; (ii) criteria are found whereby the success or otherwise of achieving these aims may be assessed; (iii) ways are found of measuring these criteria; and (iv) these measures are then related to measures of social factors within the institution.

181

Sociology of Education

During the past hundred years education in Britain has ceased to be the preserve of a few and has progressively become more widespread. With each succeeding generation a higher proportion of children has received education and in each generation more have stayed at school to a higher age. But still the proportion staying on beyond the minimum school leaving age, which at present stands at fifteen, remains small. Thus there is an educational pyramid with a solid majority receiving the minimum, and progressively fewer proceeding through the various stages of secondary and higher education. Although education is no longer only for an élite, entry to élite groups is through the educational channel.

The need for public education on a large scale came with Parliamentary reforms widening the franchise and creating the need 'to educate our masters'. Basically, the need was for a literate population, but more and more the need has grown for people capable of both acquiring the skills required by an increasingly complex industry and of coping with the growing complexities of modern urban living. A civilization such as ours depends on the ability of each individual to read and understand complicated instructions, to store and evaluate a mass of information, and to acquire the skills to cope with all the institutional demands encountered daily: demands to fill up intricate forms for government departments, local authorities and football pool promoters, from our employers, from our children's school and from our creditors. We have to learn how to obtain the services that we, in turn, need and to thread our way through the problems of a monetary economy. On top of this we are expected to be able to make judgments about government and local government policies and personalities and to provide not only for the present, but for our own future and for that of our children.

The aims of the educational system then have gradually become oriented towards preparing the children and adolescents to cope with these demands. At the same time the paths towards financial and social advancement have reduced almost to one. You will not become Lord Mayor of London by running away to sea or by enlisting as a drummer-boy, and it is becoming more difficult to rise into the ranks of industrial management from the shop floor. Trade union hierarchies find it difficult to recruit their successors from men with shop floor experience, and it may not be long before here, as in America, the main road to high union office will be through the universities. Under these circumstances, 'Who gets what education?' has become of great interest to sociologists. If we set on one side the *private* sector of education (the independent and, to some extent, the direct grant schools), the educational opportunities are theoretically open equally to all, but numerous sociological enquiries have demonstrated how socio-economic class origins are related to the chances of obtaining grammar school and university education.

Among the methods of study of these phenomena one of the most interesting and rewarding, but demanding of time and patience, is that of the longitudinal cohort study. James Douglas[8] has been studying a five per cent sample of all children born during one week in March 1946, and has followed the course of their lives, charting every few years a record of their health, education and family circumstances. At each stage the handicap suffered by those from the lowest socio-economic classes grows, few enter grammar schools and of those that do, year by year fewer are in 'A' streams, fewer stay beyond 'O' levels and so on. Low socio-economic status is not once-for-all disadvantage but has an accumulative effect. There are, of course, many factors operating: poorer people tend to have larger families and children from larger families tend to have lower I.Q.s than those from small families. Furthermore, since the less intelligent tend to move down the occupational ladder, while the more intelligent move up it, there is a tendency for people in higher socio-economic classes to provide their children with an inherited genetic advantage. Then there is the question of environment. The middle-class child has a richer variety of experience, more access to books and newspapers and has more interest taken by his parents in his school work. He is more likely to have adequate facilities for studying. But, above all, the values of the home are more likely to be oriented towards education and congruent with those of the school. Without necessarily consciously realizing it, our schools purvey middle-class values, and teachers, who are by occupation middle class, represent these values. Thus the school does not create a dilemma for the middle-class child, but the working-class child is faced with a set of values to which those of his home environment may be alien or even hostile. Numerous studies have shown the effect of these factors.

The mechanisms by which these factors affect the child and are transmitted to him have been less clear, and indeed it is startling to recognize at what an early stage in life they begin to operate. Professor B. B. Bernstein has shown that the linguistic equipment which the child acquires in his earliest years affects the possibilities of his conceptual development.[9] Language is used to serve many functions. One is to enable the individual to take his place comfortably in the social groups, membership of which is important to him. Groups of this kind require an emotional consensus. The kind of linguistic expressions suited to this aim has the characteristics of what Bernstein calls a *restricted code*. Another function of language, of immense importance, is as a tool to explore the world and describe the experience obtained by such exploration. The characteristics of the linguistic expression needed for this purpose are those of an *elaborated* code. Bernstein shows how we all acquire restricted codes of one kind or another and use them in our membership of particular groups. The elaborated codes which enable us to develop and express our individual personalities and give us a framework for exploring and communicating with the world of our experience are used and learned by middle-class, but not by working-class, families and their children. It is difficult to do justice in a brief space to his findings. What is of particular interest here, however, is that this study which originated as a *pure* piece of research aimed towards explaining the phenomena we have described of the working classes' educational handicap opened up prospects of remedial action. Might it not be possible to reshape a child's linguistic equipment even after he reached nursery school age? To examine this possibility, action research projects have been initiated in schools in one of the Greater London boroughs.

Sociologists have also been interested in what goes on in the classroom and the effects of different kinds of organization both of school and of classroom. The question of school organization has been focused on the comprehensive/selective argument, and some sociologists have been influential in pressing the claims of the comprehensive system. Indeed, it may be that in this regard some have strayed beyond the boundary of respectable sociological evidence. Streaming has been another controversial topic, and here again sociologists have taken up positions, while again the quantity of convincing evidence has remained thin.

A totally different line of educational research has been concerned with the experience of pupils in their relationships with one another. Here there has been a good deal of interest in the use of sociometry. Jacob Moreno first used this in his studies of girls in reform schools, reported in *Who Shall Survive?* 1934. He asked them to choose the girls they would like to share rooms with and those they would not. When girls were grouped with those they liked their behaviour improved. This technique has been used to discover the structure of the informal groups of pupils in schools and students in higher education. In a number of studies in America it has turned out that cliques and informal groups in school correspond closely to the lines of social-class structure in the community. Teachers who, as we have said, are themselves occupying middle-class roles, have apparently little ability to judge how pupils relate to one another. They tend generally to overestimate the popularity of the children they like and underestimate that of the children they dislike. If anything, this kind of work has tended to reinforce the emphasis in American schools on social adjustment, a concern which is only just becoming at all prominent here, just as it recedes in the U.S.A. In fact, there is now a trend in American education towards greater emphasis on the academic values

185

which appear to have had their origins in the American anxieties over *Sputnik,* and the belief that Russian education was better aimed than the American at providing a scientifically-trained population.

More recently in Britain the universities have come in for the sociologists' attention. The social-class weighting of the universities was made very clear by the Robbins Report, which showed that in 1961–2 only seven per cent of undergraduates came from an unskilled and semi-skilled background, while nearly sixty per cent came from the two highest social classes (professional and managerial). There have been studies on the effects of different systems of students' residence which have tended to show that the degree to which the student responds positively to communal residence also depends to some extent on social class. Now that the universities have cast their net wider, both in terms of entry and of subjects that are thought worthy of being the subject of a university education, the strains on the universities as institutions are beginning to show. Universities, like other institutions we have described, suffer from the muliplicity of goals. First, they are strongholds of learning, they add to and protect the stock of knowledge; secondly, they provide an environment in which a student may expand his personality, his knowledge and his understanding of the world, with the aim of educating him in the full sense; thirdly, they are vocational training establishments and are answerable in this respect, too, as guardians of professional standards. Financially they are responsible through the University Grants Committee to the government; academically they retain a good deal of autonomy. As prestige institutions they are expected to uphold the established order, yet they must encourage students to question that order. They are expected to implant democratic values in their students but, by their very nature as educational institutions, they encounter great difficulty in operating as democratic institutions. The present discontent symbolized by student unrest in many countries, including Britain, has not only aroused anxiety and concern, but is a stimulus for further sociological research. Some, who cannot distinguish the role of the doctor who describes the

186

symptoms of a disease from the role of the virus or bacterium which is its causative agent, are unfortunately inclined to blame the sociologist for the unrest.

Military Sociology

The sociologist's interest in military establishments has grown from two separate roots. The first is essentially historical, deriving from the importance of the influence of the military in history. The other root has been empirical and derives very largely from studies of military morale in the United States forces in the Second World War.

Historically, the role of the military is that of organized violence in the service of the state. This sets a problem for sociologists, who tend to see conflict in terms of social structure and violence as a breakdown of social control. Thus individual violence could be treated as irrational and deviant, but violence as an instrument of social policy could not be regarded in that light. Sociologists, then, turned to certain of the obvious characteristics of professional armies. Because they have to some extent a hangover of feudal structure, their social snobberies and class bias help to preserve the social position of traditional élites. Yet the role of the military, as shown by S. E. Finer in his book, *The Man on Horseback,* 1962, has by no means always been to maintain existing groups in power. Almost any day you may open a newspaper to see an account of yet another military *coup,* representing a shift in political power which is as likely to be to the left as to the right. Because the military is a route to advancement for ambitious young men and because in many states it is virtually the only such road, other than involvement in politics directly, the military is very likely to intervene in politics as the only alternative source of leadership. In studying these phenomena the sociologist has had to struggle against his biases. Seen from modern Western society, in which civilian control of the military appears a cardinal principle of democracy, military régimes appear undemocratic, reactionary and bad. But, as we have said, such seizures of power differ. It has been suggested that the poli-

187

tical character of a *coup* varies with the rank and seniority of the officers leading it. When these are low, the programme is likely to be socialist and radical and on occasion pro-communist. Not only, then, has the military acted in traditional backward societies as a route to the emancipation of young men from low-status backgrounds; it may also function as the emancipator of peoples. But this, of course, is not its primary role. Unfortunately, studies of military revolts have been rare.

Empirical sociological studies of the military have followed in the wake of the psychologist. The First World War found use for the recently developed methods of psychological testing in classifying the ability of large masses of recruits. The U.S. Army in particular, faced with an influx of illiterate negroes whose ability could not be assessed by normal means, turned to the psychologists, who developed the famous Army Beta (non-verbal) test of intelligence. The Second World War made new demands.[10] In Britain the traditional methods of selecting officers proved inadequate. Too few young men from the traditional sources of officer recruitment were available. Group-selection techniques were developed by social psychologists and indeed form the conceptual basis from which the ideas which underlie group therapy later derived. But despite the success of psychologists in developing methods for rehabilitating the casualties of battle stress, the British Army was reluctant to encourage or permit studies of morale. By contrast, the American forces showed themselves eager for such studies and a programme was set up and ultimately reported in the five volumes of *The American Soldier,* 1949, edited by S. A. Stouffer. It is not possible to summarize all this work in a small space. Much of it was focused on leadership styles. The human relations style of leadership appeared to increase men's satisfaction and reduce the number of hostile and aggressive actions and infractions of discipline. It did not necessarily, however, lead to conscripts accepting readily all military regulations. Whatever concern officers and N.C.O.s have for the welfare of their men, they are still part of an authority system whose demands inevitably conflict with other obligations such as those the men have to their families. The closer that soldiers get to front lines the more the trappings of authority, social rank and procedure tend to be dropped, and the feeling of kinship brought by common exposure to shared risks contributes to the mystique of combat troops. This mystique is frequently expressed in a common hostility to non-combat units and the men at the base. One of the unexpected discoveries made by sociological enquiry was that the proportion of men effective in combat was very small; indeed, it seems that of the infantry in an attack only a minority actually fire their weapons, while, of those who do fire, the proportion who actually aim at the enemy is not large. Among fighter pilots, a highly selective and trained body indeed, comparatively few were effective in combat. The sociometric status of those who were effective was high, as was found among interceptor pilots in Korea.

One study of morale in the British Services carried out during the Second World War and published only with some difficulty, showed that pilots who were of low sociometric status tended to have higher than average accident rates. Furthermore, pilots had to live up to the role set for them by the expectations of their comrades:

> The Pilot might even find it easier to rebel against the dictates of the R.A.F. authorities than to act contrary to what his friends expected of him. What was expected of each pilot was the standard of his squadron, with a permissible latitude of behaviour according to the judgement of his particular idiosyncrasies. Jimmy indulged in aerobatics which were too low, but this was excused on the grounds 'That's just like Jimmy', whereas Bob did the same thing and his co-pilots, amazed, asked, 'What's taken old Bob today?' Jimmy was expected to indulge occasionally in deviant behaviour, Bob was not. And both knew it! It is not only the isolate who may be pushed by his relationships with his group over the bounds of safety.[11]

It is on the face of it surprising that the pattern of organization of a military unit varies little with the type of task of the unit: the same ranks in the same proportion appear to be needed whether the task is to fight an infantry battle or to maintain a radar workshop. In the light of modern organizational theory this appears strange. However, we see that the structure of military organization has its rationale in the function of maintenance of internal control, and in organizational design this requirement appears to have acquired overriding precedence in the services. Yet there is much evidence for its dysfunctional characteristics in, for example, trade training units. In Royal Air Force apprentice schools, for example, the pyramidal rank structure and the allocation of different training functions to different groups of officers and N.C.O.s often means that decisions about a student had to be referred to a high level at which the student is not well known. The proliferation of ranks made a rational allocation of responsibility difficult and the conflicting demands made on the student by the different functional groups of staff all conduced to low morale among both staff and students. Sociological studies of the organization of military units are scarce, but with the opening up of the military to sociological enquiry we may expect to see interesting developments.

Sociology of Development

Fifty years ago the famous German sociologist Max Weber initiated one of the most influential approaches to the study of economic development. He was interested in the origins of European capitalism and he observed that the countries in which modern capitalism had been born and flourished were the Protestant countries of northern and western Europe. He reviewed the historical evidence and was struck by the possibility that the philosophy of the reformed religion was one which put a much greater emphasis on individual responsibility for achieving salvation than did the philosophy of the old (Catholic) religion. He examined in great detail what he came to describe as the *Protestant ethic* and showed how the kind of upbringing that a child would receive in a culture of a Protestant country would tend to make him more oriented towards commercial success than his contemporary in a Catholic country. His great work, *The Protestant Ethic and the Spirit of Capitalism,* translated in 1930, remained for a long time a piece of *pure* theory rather than the basis for practical approaches to modern development.

Another *pure* approach to these problems has been represented by the development of the work of Talcott Parsons.[12] Parsons developed a framework for analysis of social systems in which he identified four functions which were essential to every social system. These are the *G, A, I* and *L* functions. The *G,* or goal attainment, function implies that each social system exists to attain certain objectives and must develop methods for setting and attaining its goals. If the society we are speaking of is the whole nation, then the *G* system will be identical with the political system of the country. An *A* system is concerned with the methods of adaptation that the system must undergo in order to attain its goals. This machinery must be capable of supplying the necessary facilities to attain various goals at various times in various situations. While not identical with administrative machinery, it obviously includes it. The *I* system is concerned with the integration of the units of society in the process of pursuing the goals. These units may be individuals, families and other social groupings, including industrial establishments. In an industry, for example, integration is carried out by the organization of the firm. The *L* system is concerned with latent pattern maintenance and tension management. The social system is governed by a set of values which have to be accepted by people in the system. If the social system is not to disintegrate, there has to be some way of preserving its values and making sure that individuals accept them and conform to their requirements. This is undertaken principally by the family and other educational institutions which provide the system with a supply of members who are socialized to its goals.

Neil Smelser, in *Social Change in the Industrial Revolution,* 1959, applied this system of analysis to the development of the cotton industry in nineteenth-century Britain. He started his analysis with the system of manufacture of the mid-eighteenth century when cotton was mainly produced as a cottage industry which fitted the structure of the family and the community at the time. This led to bottlenecks in production, and an imbalance between spinning, carried out in the masters' sheds, and weaving, still carried out on the cottagers' hand looms. Furthermore, the cotton masters were unable to control their work people adequately under a system where work was 'put out' to them. Expanding markets for cotton textiles aggravated the situation. The success of Wesleyan Methodism among the working class, with its emphasis on sanctification through, among other things, hard work and sober habits, provided a system of values which enabled the responsibility for the difficulties to be laid at the door of the workers, who naturally enough did not always succeed in living up to these ideals. The outcome of all this was the development of the factory system and the successive introduction of the 'spinning jenny', water frame, loom, power loom and steam engine. Each of these required organizational changes to accommodate it. This had an enormous impact on the role of the family, which had hitherto managed to act as an economic unit. The family had now to provide the basis of the four functions to which we have referred to fit a factory situation. It had to provide the G function of motivation appropriate to the work; the A function, whereby family income was used to generate this motivation; the I function of organization of family roles; and the L function of socialization and tension management. The changing demands on the family made by the industry as it developed had a disorienting effect on the family, which had to adjust to a new set of functions. Smelser shows at considerable length how this took place and how auxiliary institutions, such as trade unions, emerged and focused upon themselves the functions which the family could no longer provide.

Thus, from both the work of Max Weber and that of Talcott Parsons and N. J. Smelser, we are equipped with frameworks of analysis for the sociological processes involved in industrialization and development. Strangely enough, these have not been as influential as they should have been. The problems of development have posed themselves as economic and political rather than as social, and the people called on to advise the governments of developing countries have been mainly economists and technologists. The influential texts have been those by economists such as W. W. Rostow,[13] whose five stages of economic growth are not related to stages of social organization. Thus the sociologist has been forced into the role of destructive critic rather than of technocratic right-hand man. Yet it has become obvious that the impediments to economic growth have been just as much social as economic, if not more so. The most striking social problem has been that of population growth. As the economists have shown, economic growth must keep ahead substantially of population growth if development is to occur. Yet the first impacts of Western aid in the form of medicine and hygiene have been to reduce the death rate while doing nothing to inhibit the birth rate. Thus, the populations of developing countries have been increasing at an alarming rate. The economic and technical problems of controlling population growth are trivial; the political, social and religious ones are enormous at the national level and even more serious at the local level. Thus an otherwise successful programme for persuading women to fit loops in Indian villages failed because the role of the midwives had been forgotten. Their livelihood depended on women giving birth and it was an easy matter for them to persuade women that the loops were harmful; but, really, there is no excuse for forgetting midwives or any other social group. Enough is known about the structure and function of social groups for these to be taken into account. Yet, even in such a simple matter as the provision of pure water the same kind of problem is encountered. Wells were dug in a village and villagers shown how to use them and taught the value of a clean water supply. Five months later the wells were blocked and disused and the villagers were drinking the polluted water of the river once more. It doesn't take advanced technical knowledge to maintain a well, but it does take some technical knowledge and it requires organization and training, neither of which existed and neither of which had been given a thought by the experts in the case in mind. The water supply

193

of a village, just as much as the latest automatic factory, is a sociotechnical system, and this lesson is only slowly being learned. In our concluding section we shall discuss some of the reasons why information of a sociological nature may be available but not used.

Yet another piece of pure research has turned out to have applications in the fields of development. David McClelland of Harvard University studied the relationship of achievement motivation to economic growth; his work is reported in *The Achieving Society*, 1961. He suggested that the seeds of achievement motivation were sown in the stories told to children. Our culture heroes may be the boy who, by his own exertions, has climbed from log cabin to White House, or he may be the youngest brother of the folk tale who, through kindness to beggars, is rewarded with the kingdom and the hand of the beautiful princess. McClelland showed that the former type of culture hero was characteristic of economies about to grow; the latter of economies stagnating or declining. In a recondite extension of his searches, he even scanned the pottery of pre-literate cultures to determine the degree of achievement motivation demonstrated in the styles of vase decoration and tried to show that historically the great bursts of discovery and exploration coincided with changes in complexity and originality of design. Be that as it may, he has made a strong case linking the degree of achievement motivation displayed among young people and the degree of economic development in a country. His comparative studies of managers in different countries has linked their achievement motivation to the progressiveness of industrial management. These studies, pure in their original orientation, have resulted in attempts at application. If, indeed, achievement motivation is crucial in development, can it be successfully implanted in children and in adults? Training in achievement motivation has now been tried with managers in various developing countries, including India and Mexico, and these experiments have been moderately encouraging. Certainly a link between motivation and development has been confirmed by other studies. D. Sinha has shown how motivation differs between the inhabitants

194

of backward villages in India and those of more progressive ones. The quality of leadership also varies from community to community and here again numerous studies have related the quality of leadership to the successful introduction of change. A. H. Niehoff has tested these processes in countries as far apart as the Philippines and Rhodesia and as different in culture as Taiwan and Peru.[14] There is really no further doubt about the possibilities of utilizing sociological knowledge at the micro-level; at the level of central planning, however, the story is different. We know how to draw up economic plans, but so far social planning is proving a chimera.

The Sociologist as Change Agent

At the beginning of this chapter we tried to draw out the distinction between *applied* sociology and applying sociology. There have always been sociologists interested in solving social problems or initiating social change, and much of the solid social research of the nineteenth century had, as its motive, the improvement of the lot of the underprivileged or improving the administration of social welfare. The studies of Charles Booth and B. Seebohm Rowntree into the conditions of the poor are outstanding examples. This kind of study did result in both greater understanding, and administrative change. The channel for this change was through the addition to the stock of knowledge at the disposal of Members of Parliament, senior civil servants and others interested in promoting social welfare.

In general, research gets into use by four methods. First, by the addition to the stock of knowledge and its *diffusion through general channels*. This results in time in a change in the climate of opinion which makes reform possible. It is easy enough to illustrate important and significant changes in opinion and less easy to trace these back to the results of research or to show that it was the research which did the trick. My favourite example is to contrast the mechanistic model of the worker as a factor of production whose failure led to the initiation of research by the Health of Munitions

Workers' Committee (1915) with the views held today. Even the most antediluvian contributor to the correspondence columns of *The Times* on the subject of Backing Britain can hardly still imagine that there is a linear relationship between hours of work and output. Yet the discovery that this was not the case not only came as a stupefying blow in 1915, it also led to the initiation of the long line of research into hours and conditions of work, methods of payment, etc., which laid the basis for so much of what is now standard management practice.

At the time, this was a deliberate application of research. So it is not by any means easy to draw clean lines dividing the ways in which research gets applied. The time taken for the critical change in opinion in this case was only a few years; in the more general case it may be anything up to fifty, which is, of course, too slow. Courses for managers are now the most common source of this change of opinion in industry. With their growth, the rate of change will accelerate. Courses are, of course, an excellent example of the second method whereby research becomes applied: *diffusion through special channels*. This is more rapid than diffusion through general channels, but scarcely less chancy. The third method is through *diffusion of practices*. Agricultural extension workers, factory inspectors, management consultants and managers changing employment from one firm to another convey practices observed or learned in one setting to another. Here lies the danger. What is effective in one situation may be disastrous in another. At the beginning of the chapter we mentioned how a change in any system must be seen in its effect on, and relations to, all the relevant sub-systems. If this is true for the introduction of any change, it is most crucial for a deliberate change in organization, and the application of the results of social science research are very likely to imply organizational change. The clumsy introduction of incentive payments systems is, I suspect, the most common misapplication of social science research brought about in this way.

The fourth method is by *deliberate planned application*. Here we are usually concerned with the application of specially commissioned research. Because such research has to be commissioned and paid for and is not cheap, the sponsor is likely to be a government department or an industrial firm or a major institution of some kind. This brings in its train a new set of problems. Take the industrial example: it is obviously far more likely that research will be commissioned by the management of an industrial company than by its workers or by a trade union representing them. This presents the sociologist with an ethical problem: can he be sure that the results of his work will not be misused? Can he be sure that it will not be used in such a way as to obtain workers' compliance with the objectives of management, regardless of whether this is in their true interest? Another type of ethical problem, less obvious, concerns the sociologist's relationship to his colleagues. There have been examples of sociologists who have promised more than they can perform, with the result that the sponsoring organization has been unwilling to give support to the work of other sociologists.

Project Camelot points yet another pitfall.[15] Here the United States Department of Defence and the United States Army sponsored a major study whose aim was to find out what conditions led to internal wars in states (insurgency or civil war) and how such clashes could be prevented. The directors of the project decided to make a study of Chile but their intentions leaked out to social scientists in Chile itself. The latter became alarmed and alerted their government, with the result that the United States Army repudiated the research and withdrew support. Many social scientists in the United States objected to the implications of, and assumptions underlying, the whole study. In particular, they could not agree with the assumption that insurgency and revolt are necessarily pathological: an assumption that would make the origins of the U.S.A. doubtful, to say the least. Quite apart, however, from the moral and scientific issues involved, the outcome is to make Chile and probably other Latin American countries hostile for some time to come to even the purest and best intentioned sociological research undertaken from a base in a foreign country. Another example is the Moynihan Report, 'The Negro Family: A Case for

197

National Action'.[16] This study was concerned with the basic structural sources of the disadvantages under which the negroes in the United States suffer. As a result of his investigation, Moynihan called for a thorough-going policy-planning approach to eliminating the basis of their disadvantages. The report led to a major controversy among groups interested in civil rights. To begin with the findings were misused; the evidence they provided on the instability of negro families was prayed in aid by lawyers defending school boards pursuing policies of segregation against charges that they were not providing equal education for negroes. Secondly, some of the evidence was inconvenient and uncomfortable to action groups who were, as indeed the research worker was, concerned with improving the conditions of the negro. Thus there was pressure for the social scientists to tailor their findings to the strategies that the civil rights movements wished to adopt, rather than for the strategies to be tailored to the reality discovered by the social science investigation. So undesirable moral pressure can come from both sides: from those who wish to deny the implications of the research and from those who want to use the research to support their reforming claims, but find some of the findings inconvenient or unpalatable.

The application of sociology is, therefore, not a simple matter; nor is it the right activity for a not very bright sociologist. It requires familiarity with the concepts and methods of social science and the ability to make use of a wide range of quantitative methods. It requires the understanding of the organizations or institutions in which changes are to be introduced and it also requires the ability to translate problems from one frame of reference (that of organizations) to another (that of the sociologist). Lastly, it requires patience and a tolerance of frustration greater than that needed for academic research.

SUGGESTED READING

BATES, A. P., *The Sociological Enterprise* (Boston: Houghton Mifflin Co., 1967).

APPLIED SOCIOLOGY

CHERNS, A. B., 'The Uses of the Social Services' in *Human Relations*, Vol. 21, No. 4, 1968.
LAZARFELD, P. F., *et al., The Uses of Sociology* (New York: Basic Books, 1968).
SHOSTAK, A. B. (ed.), *Sociology in Action: Case Studies in Social Problems and Directed Social Change* (Homewood, Illinois: Dorsey Press, 1966).

NOTES

1   Tavistock Pamphlet No. 7 (Tavistock Publications, 1966).
2   *On the Shop Floor* (Pergamon, 1963).
3   *The Management of Innovation* (Tavistock Publications, 1960).
4   E. L. Trist *et al., Organizational Choice* (Tavistock Publications, 1963).
5   The effect this has on his relationship with his family is noted in the work of Elizabeth Bott, *op. cit.*
6   This has been described in many accounts of the life of inmates of the German concentration camps in the Second World War.
7   *Institution and Outcome* (Pergamon, 1967).
8   *The Home and the School* (MacGibbon & Kee, 1964).
9   See *The Penguin Survey of the Social Sciences*, edited by J. Gould (Penguin Books, 1965).
10 See A. B. Cherns, 'War and Social Sciences' in *New Society*, 39, June 1963.
11 T. Paterson, *Morale in War and Work* (Parrish, 1955).
12 *The Social System* (Tavistock Publications, 1950).
13 *The Stages of Economic Growth* (Cambridge University Press, 1960).
14 C. M. Arensberg and A. Niehoff, *Introducing Social Changes* (Chicago: Aldine, 1966).
15 *The Rise and Fall of Project Camelot*, edited by O. L. Horowitz (Cambridge, Mass.: M.I.T. Publications, 1967).
16 L. Rainwater and W. L. Yanzey, *The Moyniham Report and the Politics of Controversy* (Cambridge, Mass.: M.I.T. Publications, 1967).

Appendix I

Courses offered in British Universities

APPENDIX I

COURSES OFFERED IN BRITISH UNIVERSITIES

Combined Honours Courses

University	Degree	Length, Years	Types of Courses. Single or Combined Joint Honours	Anthropology	Econ. Hist.	Economics	Geography	History	Law	Philosophy	Politics	Psychology	Social Admin.	Statistics	Theology	No. of G.C.E. A Levels Required	Named O Levels
England																	
BATH	B.Sc.	3	S. & J.H.				✓								✓	3	English, Maths
BIRMINGHAM	B.Soc.Sc.(E.P.S.)	3	J.H.		✓	✓		✓		✓	✓	✓	✓			3	Maths
BRADFORD	B.A. B.Sc.	3	J.H.			✓		✓		✓	✓	✓				2	
BRISTOL	B.Sc.(Soc.Sc.)	3	J.H.		✓	✓					✓	✓				2 or 3	Maths
BRUNEL	B.Tech.	4	C.H.		✓	✓					✓	✓				2	Maths
CAMBRIDGE	B.A.	3	Tripos (Part II)	✓		✓						✓			✓	2 or 3	Maths or Science, Foreign Language
CITY	B.Sc.	3	C.H.													2	English, Maths (pref.)
DURHAM	B.A.	3	C.H.			✓				✓		✓				2 or 3	Maths
EAST ANGLIA	B.A. (Soc.St.)	3	J.H.	✓	✓				✓							2 or 3	Maths
ESSEX	B.A. (Soc.St.)	3	S.H.					✓			✓					2	Maths
EXETER	B.A. (Soc.St.)	3	S.H. & C.H.		✓				✓	✓	✓	✓		✓	✓	3 pref.	Maths, Foreign Language, History (pref.)
HULL	B.A. (Soc.St.)	3	S.H. & J.H.	✓			✓		✓	✓	✓	✓			✓	2 or 3	English
KEELE	B.A.	3	S.H. & Dip.				✓		✓		✓		✓			2 or 3	Maths
KENT	B.A. (Soc.Sc.)	3	S.H. & C.H.		✓	✓			✓	✓	✓		✓			2	Maths
LEEDS	B.A.	3	S.H. & C.H.			✓	✓			✓	✓					3 pref.	Maths, History (pref.)
LEICESTER	B.A. (Soc.Sc.) / B.Sc.	3	S.H.					✓				✓				3	
LIVERPOOL	B.A. (Soc.Sc.)	3	S.H.													3 pref.	Maths or Latin or Greek
LONDON:																	
Bedford College	B.A. B.Sc. (Soc.)	3	S.H.													2	Foreign Language
L.S.E.	B.A. B.Sc. (Soc.)	3	S.H.													2 or 3	Maths, Foreign Language

Institution	Degree	Years	Honours	No. of A-levels	Required subjects
LOUGHBOROUGH	B.Sc. (Soc.Sc.)	3	J.H.	2	—
MANCHESTER	B.A. (Econ.)	3	S.H. & C.H.	2	Maths (pref.), English
NEWCASTLE	B.A. (Soc.St.)	3	C.H.	2 or 3	—
NOTTINGHAM	B.A. (Soc.)	3	S.H.	2 or 3	Maths
READING	B.A. (Soc.)	3	S.H. & C.H.	3	
SALFORD	B.Sc. (Soc.St.)	3	S.H. & C.H.	2 or 3	Maths, English
SHEFFIELD	B.A. (Econ.)	3	S.H. & C.H.	3 pref.	Maths, English
SOUTHAMPTON	B.Sc. (Soc.Sc.)	3	C.H.	3 pref.	Maths
SURREY	B.Sc.	3	S.H. & J.H.	2 or 3	Maths
SUSSEX	B.A. (Soc.St.)	3	S.H. & J.H.	2	—
YORK	B.A. (Soc.Sc.)	3	S.H. & C.H.	2 or 3	—
Northern Ireland					
BELFAST (Queen's Univ.)	B.Soc.Sc.	3	C.H.	2 or 3	English
ULSTER (Coleraine)	B.Sc.	3	S.H.	2 or 3	Maths (pref.), Foreign Language (pref.)
Scotland					
ABERDEEN	M.A.	4	S.H. & J.H.	2 or 3	Maths, English and Foreign Language
EDINBURGH	M.A.	4	S.H. & J.H.	3	Maths, English and Foreign Language
GLASGOW	M.A.	4	C.H.	2 or 3	Maths, English and Foreign Language
STIRLING	M.A.	4	J.H.	2 or 3	Maths, English and Foreign Language
STRATHCLYDE	M.A.	4	S.H. & J.H.	3	Maths, English
Wales					
ABERYSTWYTH	B.Sc. (Econ.)	3	J.H.	2 or 3	English or Welsh
BANGOR	B.Sc. (Econ.)	3	S.H. & C.H.	3	Maths (pref.), Eng. or Welsh
CARDIFF	B.Sc. (Econ.)	3	S.H.	2 or 3	Maths, English or Welsh
SWANSEA	B.Sc. (Econ.)	3	C.H.	2 or 3	Maths (pref.)

Appendix II

Careers in Sociology

This note is intended to give some help to people who want to know what work they could expect to get as a result of obtaining a first degree (B.A., B.Sc., etc.) in sociology. The answer depends very much on personal circumstances. There are an enormous variety of jobs for which sociology has some relevance, and which a graduate in sociology could hope to get, sooner or later. But there are only a few sorts of posts that very many graduates in sociology actually aim for. Dr Joan Abbott carried out a survey of those who graduated in 1966, and found that about a quarter aimed at becoming professional sociologists, another quarter went into school-teaching and about fifth went into social work. No other sort of employment accounted for many of the 1966 graduates. So we may as well start by considering the three large fractions.

Professional Sociologists

Sociology is a field of study rather than a field of practice; sociologists are more like physicists than engineers, and more like physiologists than doctors. That does not mean that sociologists cannot influence practical affairs, but it does mean that their professional work is mainly study (including research) and teaching.

Most research in sociology is done by people holding teaching posts. There are some research positions that do not involve teaching duties as well, but they are too few for anyone to be able to rely on getting one. They are scattered thinly among governmental and international agencies and even more thinly among business companies and voluntary organizations. They require the same kinds and levels of qualification as teaching posts do, and it is probably best to think of them as a variant on a teaching career. There are other careers based on research, and we shall consider them later, but they usually entail moving away from the main concern of sociology and some form of management.

Sociology is taught at universities, colleges of technology and further education, and teacher training colleges, and the number of posts has increased enormously in the last few years, but so has the number of applicants! Even during the period of greatest demand for teachers, jobs have tended to go to people with higher degrees (M.A., M.Sc., and Ph.D.) or substantial experience elsewhere, rather than to those who had only just received their first degree. In Dr Abbott's survey, most of those aiming to become professional sociologists went on to take higher degrees.

Courses for these degrees usually take two or three years, and they are only open to people whose first degree was of a good standard. They usually include a combination of advanced teaching and supervised research work, ranging from nearly all research in most Ph.D. courses to nearly all teaching in some M.A. and M.Sc. courses. Grants are awarded, mainly by the Social Science Research Council, to support students on these courses, but graduates are not automatically eligible for a grant. The allocation of grants is rather complicated, but from the student's point of view, the long and short of it is that if you have a first-class or upper second-class honours degree you are likely (but not certain) to be able to get a grant; if you have a lower second-class or third-class honours degree you will probably not get a grant (but you might, if you are very persuasive).

So, although most sociology graduates who want to become professional sociologists do so, there is some competition, both for higher degree courses and for jobs and, if you aim for a career in professional sociology, you should also consider in advance what your second choice of career would be.

School-teaching

Information about teaching as a career is easily available, and in this note it is only necessary to point out one or two aspects that particularly concern sociologists.

Sociology is taught in very few schools, and it cannot be taken for granted that it will spread fast. So graduates in sociology must be prepared to spend most of their time teaching other subjects. If you are at the point of choosing a university course, with a view to teaching in schools, you might well consider one of the many degrees in which sociology is combined with another subject; most of the combinations offered are with 'arts' subjects, but it is possible in some universities to study sociology and mathematics, statistics or a science. But sociology can itself give valuable new perspectives on most subjects that are taught in schools; it need not be regarded merely as a private hobby.

It is sometimes possible for a graduate to get a teaching post in a school without any qualifications beyond his degree, but it is nowadays almost essential to take a teaching qualification as well; the shortest courses for graduates last for one year. Grants have usually been easily obtained by people accepted for these courses.

Social Work

Social work means as a rule employment in one of the welfare services run by the state or local authorities. The largest groups are child care officers, probation officers, medical and psychiatric social workers, and family case-

205

workers. There is at present a very heavy demand for social workers, and it is possible to get jobs in some areas with no qualification beyond a first degree. But anybody who intends to make a career in social work should take a professional qualification. It is possible for graduates in sociology to gain a professional qualification after one year's postgraduate training, but only in certain courses; more often it takes two years. There are many different arrangements for training, and different sorts of grant are available, some bigger than others. You should get up-to-date information from the Social Work Advisory Service, 26 Bloomsbury Way, London W.C.1.

However, social work is not the same thing as sociology, or even applied sociology. Sociology is certainly one of the relevant background subjects for social work, but if you are interested in social work you should also consider the other social science degrees open to you, especially those in social administration.

Other Careers

Beyond these three popular fields of work, there is a very wide range of jobs that can be done, successfully and enjoyably, by graduates in sociology. But there are always other degree courses that provide a suitable background for any particular job, and you should consider the alternatives as closely as you can. Among the kinds of work which sociology is particularly relevant for, there are various branches of social research, management, and mass communication. Social research is usually the measurement of 'public opinion', whether about political issues or about particular goods and services, and it is carried out by such organizations as the Government Social Survey, B.B.C. Audience Research, and town-planning departments, and by many market research companies. Although this work is primarily aimed at solving practical problems, it can also provide opportunities for refining sociological theory and methods.

Management is of course necessary in all organizations, and although it demands skills that are not taught in sociology courses, there are several sociological concerns, such as the structural problems of organizations, the development of professionalism and bureaucracy, and the behaviour of groups in conflict, which are clearly important in management. One particular branch of management, personnel management, is sometimes considered different (in some ways more like social work), but this is a very questionable view.

'Mass communication' calls to mind press and television, journalists or advertisers, but there is also room for sociological understanding in the management of campaigns to improve public health, literacy, farming methods and so on. These are usually run by governments, with the support of U.N. specialized agencies.

Sometimes two or all three of these kinds of work can be combined in a single career, for instance, marketing. But all these jobs have some important features in common:

1. There are not very many posts available in them (except for industrial management); you have to go out and find one for yourself.

206

2. They are not well-trodden career paths, though you may get a start on one of them by taking one of the more exotic combined honours degrees; they are more affected by your own personality (and by sheer good or bad luck) than a career in professional sociology, school-teaching, or social work is likely to be.

3. They involve working mainly with people who are not sociologists, and they demand a primary interest in operating problems rather than academic disciplines. The sociologist may be a minor partner in a working team dominated by another professional group. He will have to translate his sociological insights and findings for his colleagues and may have to abandon lines of enquiry which are sociologically interesting but not particularly relevant to the team's task. But this situation can be expected to improve gradually as the value of the sociologist's contribution becomes apparent to his non-sociologist colleagues; provided, of course, that the sociologist plays fair by taking an interest in their contributions too.

4. They nearly always demand a good understanding of the fundamental ideas of statistics. For various reasons, some of them good ones, the sociologist may not wish to use statistical techniques in a particular job, but he will usually have to cope with searching questions from people who think he should have used them.

There is also likely to be an increasing need to understand other, non-statistical, mathematical ideas; computer languages are one obvious example.

Very many people are terrified by mathematics and statistics, but there is no need to be. If you are intelligent enough to get into a university, you are intelligent enough to learn as much maths as you need, and in the long run you can hardly afford not to learn it.

Working Conditions, Pay and Prospects

There is not very much that can usefully be said about what sort of life a sociologist leads. He is unlikely to be very poor or very rich, but if one tries to be more specific one can at best only describe current situations and 'trends', and the prospective student is really asking what conditions would be like five years from hence to fifty years hence. Nobody knows what they will be like, but it is fairly safe guess that they won't be like present conditions. They will probably continue to differ from one job to another, so that if you are determined to work odd hours or live in an odd place, you will probably be able to arrange it. But only you can discover what conditions are acceptable to you and what are not, so you should lose no opportunity of reading about jobs you are interested in, talking to people who are doing them already, doing relevant work in vacations, if possible, and perhaps doing a year's relevant work before starting your training.

However, remember that many careers include several distinct phases involving quite different sorts of work, according to experience, seniority, and changing circumstances. Although your choices now are important, they need not be irrevocable.

207

Index